SHINE!
Inspirational Stories of Choosing Success Over Adversity

Volume 4

Prominence Publishing

Book and Cover design by Prominence Publishing. www.prominencepublishing.com

SHINE Volume 4/Multiple Authors -- 1st ed.

ISBN: 978-1-988925-76-9

Table of Contents

Introduction

When I take the time to reflect on all of the authors that we have worked with at Prominence Publishing over the last 10 years, I am overwhelmed with gratitude. Every single person has touched my life in some way. What I love most about the Shine! series of books is having the opportunity to share stories with our readers that illustrate strength, resilience and above all, courage.

With that in mind I am both proud and pleased to introduce you to this incredible group of authors, who not only took time to write their stories for you but genuinely share their emotions. Every chapter of this book tells a story of someone who faced adversity, and instead of quitting, they chose courage and kept going. Regardless of their circumstances, they chose to make life-altering decisions with honor and integrity.

Please join me as you feel and experience their stories and celebrate their journeys.

Wishing you all the best,

Suzanne Doyle-Ingram

CEO, Prominence Publishing &

Creator of The Expert Author Program

"You may encounter many defeats, but you must not be defeated. In fact, it may be necessary to encounter the defeats, so you can know who you are, what you can rise from, and how you can still come out of it."

~ Maya Angelou

CHAPTER ONE

From Frustrated and Overwhelmed to Positive and Balanced

By Susan J. Ryan

I love life, being happy, and being nice.

The last thing I do before going to sleep is to review what I'm grateful for. The first thing I do when I wake up is to say thank you for the opportunity to live another day from a place of gratitude. I then move fearlessly into what my day brings, knowing I'll be a better person by the end of the day and, if the by-product of even one thing I do makes a positive impact in someone else's life, it's like hot fudge on my ice cream!

I've created the career of my passion. In roles as a speaker, coach, mentor, educator, and author, I guide individuals to feel great about themselves, make wise choices, and live satisfied with their success in each aspect of their lives.

Sometimes people question how I stay positive and balanced, even during times of extreme challenge. I welcome and understand their question because it's one I used to ask others who seemed so positive and balanced when I definitely wasn't. I invite people into the consideration of what I've learned – and continue to learn – smiling inside because it's a reminder I no longer question it in myself.

For many years, my naturally positive disposition was periodically challenged by an overwhelming feeling like something was missing in my life and not knowing what it was. I was constantly striving to be 'the best', to please others, and be 'successful' because it's what I was supposed to do.

I intentionally put quotation marks around 'the best' and 'successful'. I'd been told over and over they were what I should strive for, but I hadn't defined them for myself. I assumed others knew and if I asked them their definition, they would know I didn't know.

I've learned this was a huge mistake and that, just like me, few people have defined these words with clarity for themselves. Tip – I've become unquenchably curious about having clarity on the definition and meaning of words I'm using. This is tremendously helpful for me in staying positive and balanced. In conversations with others, I now make sure our definitions are aligned. Hint: Start with the definition of the word 'guilty'.[1] Do its definition and meaning match yours? What word/phrase serves you more accurately?

---

[1] https://www.merriam-webster.com/dictionary/guilty

Whenever I took on a project I worked as hard as I could, so I'd be 'the best' or 'successful', and I've achieved the highest recognition in many aspects of my life. Rather than feeling great about myself, living my positive and balanced life satisfied with my success, I was often exhausted, frustrated, and overwhelmed and almost always felt like I'd missed the mark.

Of course, I felt this way. It's like trying to hit a piñata blindfolded!

I had a profound defining moment that began my transformation. I'm now able to repurpose earlier life lessons that remind me I do have a choice. It's actually the word choice that began the transformation.

My Defining Moment

Driving home from the memorial service for one of my best friends who had died after a brave battle with cancer, I became aware that I accepted her death and that it was meant to teach me something in my life. This was a new awareness[2] for me. I wasn't sure what to do with it so, as a person of faith, I asked God for guidance.

Several days later, driving to work, it was as though someone was in the back seat of my car and said out loud, "Choice". Immediately I had an understanding that no matter what my friend did in her life, the choice was taken away from her and each day when I woke up, I still had a choice. The question that accompanied this understanding was "How are you going to use choice?"

---

[2] http://www.simplifyinginterfaces.com/2008/08/01/95-percent-of-brain-activity-is-beyond-our-conscious-awareness/

One Choice

I begin and end my day from a place of gratitude. Gratitude opens me up to potential and possibilities in every situation. It's choosing to seek what there is for me to learn and use it to improve my life and the lives of others.

Here's one of my favourite quotes on gratitude:

"Gratitude is when memory is stored in the heart and not in the mind."

– Lionel Hampton

One Repurposed Lesson

Repurposed lessons give us the opportunity to gain new insights from earlier life lessons, now that we're in different stages of our lives.

In my teen years, my Dad used to challenge me to not settle for being 'the best'. We showed American Quarter Horses and I had been winning the classes I entered. He saw that, even though my performance was good, it was not what I was capable of. Rather than tell me I was capable of more, Dad wanted me to learn to see it in myself, for myself, and guided me to challenge myself to be 'my best'. He explained, "It's more important for you to be your best than to be the best."

I wasn't sure how to figure that out in myself. Dad explained I would recognize it when I didn't feel satisfied and I would learn how to find it from there. It was easier to try to be 'the best', and I let Dad's lesson go. Fortunately, it came back at the perfect time, repurposed, when I could clearly understand its purpose.

Years later, my sales team and I were about to be recognized for the record setting enterprise application software sales results we achieved for the year. Now, the exact time I should be feeling on top of the world, I had that familiar feeling of having missed the mark. Why wasn't I feeling satisfied and fulfilled? I was proud of our work and I'd done the right things for the right reasons. Why wasn't this enough?

Suddenly, I had a powerful insight into clarity. I could hear my Dad's challenge as if he was speaking out loud. I realized I'd been striving as hard as I possibly could to achieve success defined by someone else. Without defining it for myself and working to achieve that, no matter what I achieved, I wouldn't feel satisfied.

As I walked across the stage to accept my award, I had a happy smile on my face, and I was filled with peace and joy. I knew what was missing and what to do so I would never feel this way again. I could settle for being 'the best' or I could search inside for what being 'my best' means and live my life from there. I've come to learn sometimes they're the same and sometimes they aren't. Thanks, Dad.

Self-Mastery

I began my discovery of what's important to me, why it's important, and how to live my life through it. I learned this is self-mastery and it has amazing layers of insights.

Here are five of the most valuable insights in my journey to becoming 'my best'.

Whether these become yours or not, please promise yourself you'll continue on your journey of self-mastery and not settle for anything less than your best. You're worth it!

Self-Awareness

Research continues to confirm that at least 95% of our brain activity is unconscious. The more we focus on being aware of our thoughts, feelings, and actions, the more we consciously choose what serves us.

Beliefs

These are unconscious shortcuts we've developed to help us make sense of our world. They can support us positively or they can hold us back.

Practicing awareness, I was able to discover the source of my limiting belief about 'success' or being 'the best'. It had come from my gymnastics coach when I was 8 years old.

I loved gymnastics. One day, just before a tumbling run, my coach told me I'd never been any good. As I tumbled across the mat, I began sobbing and believing I'd never be good at something so important to me. I didn't question him; I trusted him because he was a person of authority. This became my unconscious limiting belief and for many years, without knowing it, I carried that belief with me through everything I did. I didn't know how to raise it to my awareness and reevaluate whether or not it still served me.

Become self-aware. Evaluate your beliefs. Make sure they're authentically yours. If they still serve you, great. If not, choose what does serve you.

Massive Acceptance

My dad, my hero, was diagnosed with a type of Dementia. I accepted his diagnosis and used lessons he'd taught me throughout my life to support him with love. During a challenging experience with him, I realized I'd accepted parts of his diagnosis, but I hadn't accepted it completely, absolutely, in its entirety – *massively*.

Massive acceptance eliminates judgement and the need to understand in the moment. We see clearly because we're not clouded by the past or fortune-telling what the future might be. We have access to both the experience and lessons from it – even if we don't know how we'll use them.

Radical Presence

Being vigilant and practicing massive acceptance allows us to stay thoroughly, completely, and utterly focused on exactly what's going on in the present moment. We have this focus on our thoughts, feelings, and actions. This is a *radical* presence.

My beloved husband, Jack, has Alzheimer's Disease. From the day he was diagnosed, I've said the same greeting every time I see him: "Hello love of my life, how's the man of my dreams?" He always gets a big smile on his face that brings great joy to my heart.

Practicing massive acceptance and radical presence allows me to remain fully present when we're together. I meet him where he's at in the moment, support him with clarity, and make wise choices. When it became time for Jack to move into a memory care facility and receive the care I was no longer qualified to provide, I didn't feel like I'd failed him because I couldn't care for him or that I was losing him. I made the wise choice that was the best for both of us.

This year, the pandemic added a new challenge. Massive acceptance and radical presence supported me staying positive and balanced during our 200 days apart. During this time, we navigated Jack's diagnosis of COVID-19 including a hospital stay, a month of in-room quarantining, and recuperation therapy.

Jack also transitioned away from recognizing me as his wife or knowing me by name. Accepting this as part of the progression of the disease, rather than trying to get him to recognize me, I studied what this change represents and made adjustments to support him.

I didn't cloud our experience by worrying, being angry about what had happened, or projecting what might happen. I felt the emotions that served, rather than hindered, each experience. Did I get sad sometimes? Absolutely. Was I able to feel joy during our weekly video chats? Absolutely. Did I get angry? Absolutely not – it served no purpose.

Worry

I've learned worry is a wasted emotion that sucks energy from our lives and adds no value. It's an emotion that clouds our vision and prevents us from having the correct emotion. It stops us from making wise choices, taking appropriate action, and developing resilience. It becomes a screenwriter for imagined scenario after scenario until we're confused and overwhelmed.

Practicing massive acceptance and radical presence leaves no space for worry.

Here are three tips to try if you sense yourself becoming worried.

❖ Begin with awareness you're worrying and ask yourself what emotion serves you better.

❖ Break down your concern into smaller and smaller pieces until you can identify what you actually have control over and take positive action from there.

❖ Identify how you'll know when the situation is resolved so you can have closure and move on.

With each new experience, we have the potential to quickly fall back into old and familiar patterns. I have. Please be gentle with yourself. Use these as an opportunity to learn and move yourself back into feeling positive, balanced, and satisfied. You're worth it!

About the Author
Susan J. Ryan

Sue Ryan sees a world where awakened and curious people make the positive impact they are meant to, feeling satisfied with their contributions, and living their best lives feeling fulfilled.

For nearly thirty-five years, she's been guiding business professionals to become their greatest leading themselves and others, modeling this with individuals and teams, from entrepreneurs to Fortune 100 C-Suite leaders. Through their partnership, clients have collectively recognized hundreds of millions of dollars in revenue gains and operational efficiency improvements, sales and operational teams consistently deliver results-driven and record-breaking performance, and individuals feel satisfied with their success and fulfilled through the positive impact of their contributions.

At the same time, Sue has been positively navigating roles as a caregiver for friends and family members including her grandmother, father and husband. When her first caregiving experience began, she felt frightened, overwhelmed, frustrated, and like she was on an emotional roller coaster - often blindfolded. She didn't know what to do, how to do it, or where to get help. She's learned a lot!

Sue is passionate about sharing what she's learned from so many others who have leaned in to support and guide her over the years. She does this through what she loves most - mentoring, teaching, coaching, communicating as a speaker and author.

If you're curious to learn more about how to feel great about yourself, make the positive impact you're meant to, and feel satisfied with your success, have a conversation with Sue.

Connect with Sue:

Sue@sueryan.solutions

Sueryan.solutions

https://www.linkedin.com/in/suearmstrongryan

CHAPTER TWO

Life Doesn't End in Victory Lane

By Randy Tolsma

Today I the Executive Vice President of Operations at AMCI, an automotive marketing, testing, and training company. I oversee multiple departments, numerous employees, and have traveled and worked across the globe. I have been the author of cultural initiatives, helped launch multiple automotive brands domestically and internationally, all with a high school education, zero corporate work experience, and no resume. The path to my current role is unique, unprecedented, and somewhat surreal.

When I was just 15 years old, I was a hobbyist race car driver, and was interviewed about goals and aspirations for an article in the local Meridian Speedway racing program called "Driver of the Week". This was a small, one-page interview so race fans could get to know just a little more about the drivers hidden by helmets and roll bars. In my interview, I boldly and ignorantly stated that if I was not racing the Indianapolis 500 by the time I was 30, I would quit racing. It was an audacious statement for the record, but one I honored when I celebrated my 30th birthday the day before I got on the track at the famed 2.5-mile oval called Indianapolis Motor Speedway for the first time. To add to that already lofty premonition, a few years later I remember stating that the pen and pencil set I received for my high school graduation would be saved and only used for signing autographs at Indy. In 1996 I did sign with that pen. It was mostly dry - but I signed with it anyway.

At the time I had no idea how lofty those goals were, but my 15-year-old self-believed in me. I may have been the only one because I heard from many people that the idea of making it to the hallowed grounds of Indy was unattainable. I was often told not to dream big because they didn't want to see me hurt or disappointed. All warnings were shared in love, trying to protect me from inevitable pain. But, as I heard the warnings, I also heard 3-time NASCAR Cup Champion Darrell Waltrip say, "You can do anything if you put your mind to it, anything." The funny thing was, Darrell wasn't even a hero at the time. He was loud and obnoxious and his nickname was "JAWS" because he talked non-stop. But I held onto his words, because Darrell had made it and so could I. Years later I was on the board of Motor Racing Outreach with Darrell, providing me with the opportunity to thank him for his motivation, and we became friends.

It all started on a hot summer Idaho day in 1976. My dad called me down to his welding and repair shop because he had something to show me. I was within pedaling distance, so off I went as fast as my 9-year-old legs would go. In the poorly lit back room of my dad's shop, filled with grinding dust, sitting diagonally atop a fabrication table was a purple go-kart. This kart wasn't anything fancy; it was something my dad had actually bartered for. The engine didn't sit on the side like current go-karts of the day but behind the driver. The kart had drum brakes, unlike the disc brakes on modern karts. It had no number plates, just an ugly yellow engine and white seat. The year was 1976, and this was a 1965 Rupp Kart - but it was the coolest, most beautiful thing I had ever seen. We painted it red, fixed a few things, added bumpers, and number plates, and off we went to practice at the high school parking lot. I drove around cones in my borrowed oversized metallic turquoise protective jacket with white racing stripes, while wearing my $15-dollar stars and stripes Easy Rider helmet with a blue bubble shield and white bill visor.

Weeks later, we arrived at my first race, and I immediately walked to where the trophies were displayed on top of a table. I picked up the 1st Place trophy for my division and admired it - I had never had a trophy before. I put it back, confidently waiting until I had earned it later that day. I finished 3rd in that first race, not a bad finish; but in complete transparency, there were only 3 karts racing.

I continued to race through the years, winning go-kart races until 15, then on to full-size cars by my 16th birthday. I raced locally, winning races and championships.   Each and every stage of my career has a long story about dedication, determination, perseverance, sacrifice, and support. As a married man, there were times we lived on cold cereal and paid the rent with the last bit of change to our name. For 3 years we would leave work on Friday night, drive from Boise Idaho to central California - 751 miles in 12 hours. Get up on Saturday, drive to southern California, race, and then drive home again Sunday, 31 times a year, for 3 years. We moved to Indiana after selling everything we owned. What wasn't sold was shoved into a 4'x8' Uhaul trailer and our 2 cars. I didn't do any of it alone, there is no way I could have. I was supported by many, including my incredible wife at the time, Tiffanie.

Racing treated me well and I achieved almost everything I desired, but I fell short of a few very important milestones in my career. This is where it gets emotionally hard for me. I didn't qualify for the Indianapolis 500, but in 1996 only 33 of the 5.79 billion people in the world did. I crashed on the last day of qualifying at over 228mph. I was so close, I was fast enough, but one tiny gust of ill-timed air and I lost control. I let it slip away, never having one of those rings that the starting 33 drivers receive. It sounds so simple, and so stupid to say that I was lucky enough to drive at Indy but I didn't make the race and it hurt. In the bigger picture of life, it's really quite a silly statement, but to someone who pursued something every waking moment of their life - it was a tremendous letdown.

I made it to NASCAR but never made it to the uppermost level, the Cup level. Sadly, I blew a right-front tire while testing at Homestead, FL, crashing violently, and never got the opportunity to try again. Close - so very close, but my name will never make it in the record books as a driver in the most elite levels of the sport I loved so much. How many get to the level I reached? How many win national races on live television? How many get paid to race cars? Not many but doesn't mean that it doesn't hurt.

On November 3rd, 2001, after finishing 32nd in the Sam's Club 200 Busch Grand National race in Rockingham, NC my career was basically over. It had been the most stressful season of my career, and the team and I had one more race to go before re-grouping for the 2002 season. I pulled to a stop on the pit road along the inside wall of the back straightaway. I took off my gloves, released the seat belts, pulled my helmet off, and be-gan to pull myself out of the number 25 United States Marines Chevrolet. My arms pulled me up and as my leg draped over the door and touched the ground with one foot in the car and one foot out, I was overwhelmed with the feeling that this was it, my career was over. I saw crew members walking toward me to do their various post-race jobs, and, as much as I tried to put this premonition aside, I knew that this was the last time I would make a career out of driving race cars.

Just two days later, on Monday, I was called to the shop. Since this had never happened before - and I still had the over-whelming feelings from the prior Saturday, I anticipated the outcome. Owner Ed Rensi called me into the office to tell me I would not be attending that final race as their driver. I am cer-tain Ed had much more to say that day, but I was no longer lis-tening. I had just been told my dreams were over. Combine that blow with the fact that my wife was seven months preg-nant; I was completely overwhelmed. My head was spinning, my body shaking in fear. I was in a complete fog, unable to think or function. From his office, I had to exit through the race shop to the transporter to retrieve my personal items. This meant I had to walk past my team members, who I am certain had already been informed of my dismissal earlier. It was quite possibly the most humiliating thing I have ever had to do. My team had become family, but now they turned their backs as I walked by, no longer wanting or knowing what to say. I was alone, more than I had ever felt in my life, and now I had to tell my wife I had lost my job. Not only that, I didn't have any idea where my next paycheck would come from nor how I would support our growing family.

Two distinct things stand out about that time. First, I didn't have a clue what my future held - I had no vision, plan, experience, or a past that had any relevance to help me find my next job. The only dream I had ever known in my entire life was over. This wasn't just the loss of a job; this was the loss of who I was. Racing was my identity, my passion, and the source of my confidence. I believed it was the only thing I was good at - and without it, I was an empty shell of myself. I was crushed, confused, and gutted. I was a walking empty shell with absolutely no self-worth.

When reading the above I feel like it sounds shallow. So what, I was no longer a race car driver, no longer able to pursue a dream... Few ever get the opportunity I lived for 15 years - and now I have a son about to be born. Why could I not be excited about that next chapter? I was thrilled about Elijah being on the way, but I was disappointed in myself as a father before I even became one. How would I support my growing family? I was the sole provider at the time and I no longer had a job, education, or experience in a trade to find another. I wanted my son to be proud of his dad, and before he was born, I was already failing.

A counsellor later explained the loss of racing was like the death of a loved one for me. I was bitter, sad, scared, and humiliated - which led to more anger. How could something so incredibly important be ripped from me, especially after giving everything I had to it? How could I give of myself to the extent that I did, and have it end that way? How could I walk in faith, only to be let down? Luckily my faith was strong, although certainly shaken, and I was angry at God for letting this happen. I yelled out many, many times in pain, balled up in fear, and hid away from the world.

A few years later I was asked to speak at a church, which was very common prior to ending racing, and it took everything I had to find the courage to share my story and say what I needed to say. Sadly, I was not yet over the pain and humiliation. I had given something my all and failed. I had given racing to God, and I was not blessed. But, as I began to speak, I felt as though God spoke through me, and I was finally able to feel and share my insights. Perhaps, when I was 9 years old, looking at that incredibly beautiful purple go-kart in the dirty backroom of my dad's shop, if God had said - "*I will give you the victories, not just locally but also nationally. You will make a living driving a race car. You will throw out first pitches, land on aircraft carriers, and support the troops. You will color commentate on TV, you will even get the joy of seeing replicas of the cars you've raced on shelves as Hot Wheels. But you will never make it to the top, never compete in NASCAR's highest level, or wear a ring as one of the 33 starters of the Indianapolis 500*". Would I still have pursued the dream? I had to laugh because it was silly that I achieved greater joys and success than my 9-year-old self ever could have imagined or even dare dream. So, how could I now be so angry that it was over, even if it was shy of what I wanted?

I believe most of the anger was more about fear - I had no idea what to do next. Not only did I not know what I would do, but I also had no idea who I was, where my talents lay, what hobbies I enjoyed, or what I stood for. I was humiliated because I was caught up in my identity as a race car driver and didn't believe in myself otherwise. I had no plan. I had built my foundation on the loose sand of my career as a driver and belief of who I was when driving.

What I have since learned is that business is not really that different. We set goals, even if just in our thoughts, we work to achieve them, and we often lose sight of what lead to that very first dollar we framed. Goals are important, vision is imperative for success, but we must also remember our achievements and the personal foundation those achievements were built upon.

In one of my favourite books, *Onward, How Starbucks Fought for Its Life Without Losing Its Soul* (Rodale, 2012), Howard Schultz helps paint a picture of a 1983 trip to Milan, where he had a life-defining interaction with a barista in a small café. He was mesmerized by the show, the magic, and the relationship built between the barista and his customers in moments while making a cup of espresso. He immediately recognized that this was not merely a job, but a passion for the barista. That epiphany of passion and belief lead to the building of an empire called Starbucks that spread globally. During the economic downturn in 2008, the brand he built had its 'very foundation shaken, much like mine was when racing ended. What he did then is what true leaders do - he returned boldly to the helm of his company, after stepping aside years earlier to pursue global initiatives. He went back to his original vision, to the goals he set that precipitated the meteoric rise of Starbucks. He once again stood on the foundation he himself had built and returned his dream to the very core. Howard Schultz knew exactly who he was, what he believed, and what it would take to empower the coffee giant to succeed once again.

"Success is not sustainable if it's defined by how big you become. Large numbers that once captivated me -

40,000 stores! - are not what matter. The only number that matters is "one". One cup. One customer. One partner. One experience at a time. We had to get back to what mattered most."
- Howard Schultz, Onward, p. 156

So, on a Tuesday at 5:30 pm in February, Starbucks closed all of its doors worldwide in an unprecedented move. Notes were taped to all doors stating, *"We're taking the time to perfect our espresso. Great espresso takes practice. That is why we are dedicating ourselves to honing our craft."*

Howard Schultz knew deep down exactly what the foundation of the company he built was - and got back down to basics. He had the confidence and vision to know who he was – the cornerstone of the brand and what the brand needed to reboot and rebuild.

I could never expect to be held in comparison to a leader like Howard Schultz, but I can definitely make a comparison to the difference in his actions vs. mine. Mr. Schultz took bold, decisive steps to rebuild a brand with the vision and core goals he originally built his company - all while the financial world came crumbling down in 2008. I, on the other hand, dropped my head in humiliation and walked away from a dream because I no longer knew what ground I stood on. I had lost belief in myself on how I had gotten to where I was and what I had achieved. My world had been shaken, and instead of looking into the eyes of my 15-year-old self who knew exactly what he wanted, had the confidence in himself to overcome all odds - I let the world tell me everything I was not.

Racing gave me more in life than I ever dreamed I would achieve. However, I failed to look beyond racing, even knowing it would not last forever. I focused on the NASCAR Cup division and ran right to it, but my vision did not extend beyond that - I did not prepare wisely. Sadly, it ended abruptly with nothing planned beyond that. I was 36 years old and at a complete loss. I had a wife, a newborn son, and no next steps.

Even though my foundation was shaken, I found a job working as an independent contractor for AMCI. I showed up and worked hard, once again giving it my all. I had much to learn - starting at the bottom, then growing into a job staffing all AMCI programs nationwide. Only a few years later my boss resigned, leading to conversations about his replacement, a job I did not want. I knew my skills did not match those of my predecessor, but I offered my views of the department to David Stokols, President and CEO. David listened to my views about the skills and leadership I believed would help the department I worked for. As we spoke, he asked me why I was not being interviewed for the Director role. My answer consisted mainly of how I was not qualified, and how I did not possess the necessary skills to lead the department. I did share where I thought I was gifted and why that fit me well in my current position. His response was simple - I would take the role.

I learned so much about the business and myself over those few years. Constantly learning about business, but also how much I had learned on the racetrack and in life were duplicated in a pragmatic way. I had never sat in an office chair, but I had sat in the driver's seat and had learned from some amazing leaders in my racing career. Years later I took over more departments, eventually becoming a Vice President, but more importantly, I learned more about who I was.

I was a fighter determined to overcome odds, I was passionate, and I was a servant leader. I needed to have pride in who I was, and I would never have accomplished all I did without the right people believing in me. Having good cheerleaders is imperative, and I have been blessed with a few very special people in my life that have always believed in me more than I have in myself.

I encourage you to constantly remind yourself who you are, what you stand for, and what your foundation is built on. Then, when times get rocky, you know where to return to regain your foothold.

We all have plans - some spoken, some written, some just buried in our own minds, but we all have them. We work extremely hard to achieve them, and we often lose sight of the vision that got us there. We will have challenges, some bigger than others and we will be knocked down, hurting our pride and ego. It is then when we realize who we are, what we are made of and the will within.

Life doesn't end when we celebrate in victory lane, and it certainly doesn't stop when we finish defeated. So - keep fighting, learning, and planning. Regain your foothold, remember the foundation of who you are. But, also remember what your 15-year-old self would say and the attitude they would tackle life with before the world told you what was impossible.

About the Author
Randy Tolsma

Randy Tolsma lived the American dream. He grew up in Meridian, ID, and dreamed of becoming a race car driver from an early age.

His career started at age 9 in a go kart, and by 15 he was behind the wheel of a race car. He raced nearly every small oval across the western United States before moving to Indianapolis to race full time. He dabbled in Indy cars, failing to qualify for the Indianapolis 500, then on to NASCAR. He raced 500+ races in his career, throughout the United States and briefly in Europe, with national wins in NASCAR.

To stop racing was his choice. He was no longer interested in just driving for a paycheck - he wanted to win. Racing required full dedication and had a wife and newborn son. To give everything for an opportunity just to drive was not what he wanted - so he stepped out of the cockpit for good.

Walking away from that dream at 36 years old was not easy. He was lost, had no identity, passion, confidence, nor self-worth. This destructive belief harmed his relationships and self-esteem.

After leaving racing, he was offered an opportunity to work in the automotive marketing industry, re-invent himself, and build a new career. He was hired by AMCI at their corporate headquarters in Los Angeles. He soon became Vice President of Operations, and now enjoys running the day-to-day operations for a global company as Executive Vice President of Operations.

Randy is a speaker on the art of leadership and challenging the status quo. His inspirational and creative messages combined with his dynamic storytelling style make him a sought-after corporate speaker.

Connect with Randy:

RandyTolsma.com

CHAPTER THREE

The Mosquito and Me

By Christie McPhee

For my grandsons, Alex and Brad, who bring such youthful delight into my life.

My story chronicles the mundane, profound, sad, and joyous moments inspired by the loss of my son, Duncan Paul McPhee (May 23, 1985 – January 20, 2008).

Duncan inspired me and many who knew him. If his life, at 22, could get snuffed out without warning, then why would I not live the rest of my life to the fullest and be present and grateful for every second of it?

I write this in the hopes of shining a light for those on the path behind me...

October 2020.

Seven months since the pandemic has gripped our lives. I am one of the lucky ones for sure. I am healthy, I am not alone, I run a thriving home-based wellness business, and I enjoy very interesting work in the film industry. My spiritual community is sturdy and supportive. I have music in my life. I am well loved. I am truly blessed and deeply grateful for my life. All of it.

Sunday morning, January 20th, 2008, approx. 10:30 a.m.

I can't remember where I was the night before but what happened when I opened the door to my little cabin that next morning is indelibly printed on my mind.

Everything looked completely different. Had I walked into the wrong place? Did I put my contacts in the wrong way? Something was terribly amiss – I had completely lost my bearings, my sense of the norm – like I had stepped through a portal into another universe. I knew, in every cell of my body, that my whole world had changed. I just didn't know how. Yet.

Two days later. Driving along the Upper Levels Highway. Phone rings. My son's boss. "Have you seen or heard from Duncan in the last couple of days? It's not like him to not show up for work or at least call." My stomach lurched. Cold clammy sweat. Already starting to *know*. No. It wasn't like him at all. He loved his job. He was living the dream – in Whistler, off to a great start with his real estate career, skiing whenever, playing guitar at his favourite local haunts… not bad for a 22-year-old kid.

Called his cell. Voicemail full. Shit. Called his Dad and Sean. Have you talked to him? Texted friends. Smoke signals already spreading far and wide. Has anyone heard from him? Search on the mountain initiated. Police were called. Boss was given permission to break into his apartment.

Next call from his boss, "Mrs. McPhee, your son is not alive."

I remember hearing these words while I was at work. My friend Laura was there and I think she knew what I already knew. Deep, primal moans that I had to let run their course so I could do what had to be done in the next few minutes. Call his father and older brother. Call my mom. Call my meditation "buddy" so he could muster my spiritual community's support. Call more friends. Let them call the rest. Stand and watch my world come crashing to a halt. A new reality. Life as I've never known. Whirlwind, blurry, foggy, loud, quiet, weird, overwhelming, scary, all rolled up into one thing. I am at the beginning of a very long journey of loss, deep sadness, and questions. And a decision. Somehow, I knew, in those first moments that I had to make a choice. For the rest of my life, I could mourn the loss of my son or I could forge a relationship with him in spirit. Starting immediately. The sense of calm (albeit temporary) was palpable. I knew I had lost him, but I also knew I would find my way to knowing he was around me eventually. It was just a thread of belief, but one I clung to in those first months of abject grief.

What happened next haunts me and I'm not sure I have ever told my son, Sean, how deeply sorry I am for thinking he could drive us all the way to Whistler so we could meet with the coroner. He did, and how he did, I will never know. He had just lost his brother and that he would have been in shock too didn't register for me until the next day. Sean, I am so sorry. And so grateful. I didn't want anyone other than the three of us to do that torturous drive. I will never forget you on that night. So brave. So strong. So you.

The wait for the coroner was interminable. I just needed to know the cause of death. Endless possibilities ran through my mind – some of them so unbelievable that I couldn't say them out loud. I don't remember much else other than the incredible grace and compassion she had when she gave us the news – cardiomyopathy. Died peacefully.

Knowing he had passed a couple of days earlier, I wasn't sure I was up to seeing him one last time. I actually wanted to remember him as I'd seen him last – playing guitar and smiling. His Dad did want to see him and Sean was unsure. To my relief, the decision was taken out of our hands – we were advised not to. Very hard to hear and very final.

This was starting to feel real. Really real.

The next few days were a blur. I do remember going to my meditation class and sitting there trying to contain an internal earthquake. I was shaken to the core. And there were so many willing friends and family to help absorb the shock.

And then the world chimed in. Calls from family back east and a friend in Australia, a temporary shrine built at Angkor Wat in Cambodia – his picture and candles adorning a busy sidewalk while strangers walked by paying homage to a young boy they had never met, and a beautiful message from his uncle and cousin who were travelling in Switzerland – stopping at a chapel to honour his memory.

I literally could fill this book with names of people who came out of the woodwork in various forms of shock, grief, horror, love, peace, and serenity. (To this day, the memory of the many kindnesses over the next several months, years even, still brings tears to my eyes.)

The funeral. No. A Celebration of Life. Call it what you will, the value of this rite of passage was enormous. It gave us a focal point for our energy and helped ward off the fog of denial.

So many decisions that you never want to have to make. Not to go into detail, we bucked the system and did not choose package #1 or #2, or, or, or... just 1 white casket please, 22 white roses, and can we have his white guitar on a stand? Thank you. Oh yes, and we'll take that urn over there. God, really? Was this happening?

I'd wake up every morning thinking it was all a dream and then reality would hit. Again. One foot in front of the other. I knew I would make it but it was going to be a long road ahead.

How have I come from that place to where I am now? It started with a mosquito.

Day 3 of my life without Duncan. I needed to get in my car and drive somewhere. I just wanted to feel normal if only for a little while. It was a very cold and snowy day. (Of course it was. Duncan loved the snow! He was to remind us of his presence for the next few days by inundating the entire Lower Mainland with more snow than it had seen in years.) As I was starting the car, I noticed a little mosquito buzzing around in front of me. I couldn't believe this tiny thing was able to survive in the cold. I whisked him away and didn't think anything of it again. The next day I got in the car, and he was still there! I said to him (yes, I talked to the mosquito), "What are you doing here? How are you surviving without food and water (a.k.a. blood)? Who are you?"

I knew from that moment on, any mosquito that showed up, especially in challenging conditions, would be Duncan. No question. He made himself known really quickly as if to say, "Have no doubt – I am here!"

That was when I knew, regardless of how long the dark days ahead may continue, that I would come to have him and this experience in a wholesome and well way. With a lot of help.

Having always been a champion of not just physical wellness, but mental, emotional, and spiritual as well, I knew I needed to be even more conscious in all of those areas now. I had a vague sense that if I made better choices for my body, I would be creating a robust container for my tumultuous emotions and that over time, I would learn to live with my drastically-altered family reality. Mental well-being has never been an issue as I have always enjoyed a thirst for knowledge and challenges that keep me sharp and have known when to ask for help if I needed it. Spiritually, I had a long road ahead but without the support of my practice, I know I wouldn't be as well as I am today.

It has taken many years to thaw. And I do mean thaw versus melting down. It has been a slow decompression that seems to align timing-wise with what I am able to assimilate. I know this deep grief will never go away, but its presence does ebb and flow. There are times when I get blindsided by a remark or a memory that can momentarily catch me off guard, but that's understandable. What I experience more often now is a memory that will make me break into a huge grin or actual out-loud laughter. I relish these moments.

A lot of our family healing has come through music. Duncan was an inspired guitarist, and many of us (including cousins, aunts, and uncles) play. For the first few years, we hosted an annual celebration of Duncan in the form of a family-and-friends concert and fundraiser. I looked forward to those events every year knowing the incredible amount of love that would be present. It buoyed our spirits and helped keep his memory very much alive. Now with growing families and distance between the performers, it has become more challenging to host it as often, but as Shakespeare wrote, "if music be the food of love, play on", and that we do whenever we can get together.

Am I a different person because of all this? I'm not so sure. I think this has just helped to peel off a lot of unnecessary layers that I was busy creating over the years to prevent others (and myself) from knowing who I really am at heart. Part of the persona that I cultivated was so that I would be liked – or loved even. I did anything I could to avoid being criticized and wanted to be seen as an intelligent, uber-cool, successful, talented, and desirable woman. Now I am far more interested in who I am from the inside out, regardless of what others think or see. That's been the biggest shift – and the biggest gift. Fearless. Unflinching. Not afraid of death anymore. Living. Saying yes, and then figuring it out as I go along.

Do I behave differently though? Absolutely. I have a much lower tolerance for bullshit, drama, flattery, and insincerity. My appreciation for the aesthetic, silence, authentic connection, and each present moment, has grown immeasurably. (It helps to have two little grandsons running around my home as constant reminders of the wonderment of life!) The smallest things matter – both given and received. I have a new-found zest for life that is fueled by curiosity, enthusiasm, laughter, and constant learning.

And oh, the learning. I am often asked by others how I have survived what most consider to be one of the worst things that could happen to a parent. Fortunately for me, I was raised in a large family where optimism and humour were a big part of our familial philosophy. Had that not been the case, I would not have had as good a foundation for my journey.

I do know that everyone's experience is very personal and unique. I couldn't begin to tell another how to walk this path. What I willingly share are my own realizations in the hopes that they may resonate with someone in need. I firmly believe that although each of us has our own way of dealing with trauma and recovery, we all have that within us to companion our-selves – as the chestnut has everything within to become a full-grown tree, with support from the other trees in the forest.

For those of you who may not have suffered a loss such as this, but have experienced the unexpected, you too have it within you to find your footing again. Part of that is recognizing who you want to have in your life that will support you in finding that inner resource that can lead you out of the woods and back on the path.

I learned, with help, to walk towards, not away from, the pain and the memories. To breathe into the unknown. To practice gratitude. Every day. To really "get" that things happen "for" me, not "to" me. To enjoy life and know that it is okay to be happy. To know that having sadness is part of the deal but it doesn't define me.

I'm not afraid to have him in the room with me. I talk about him. Tell stories about his antics. Give others permission to talk about him too. I keep in touch with his friends and their new families. I often wonder who he might have married, had chil-dren with, and what he would look like now. I know what he would sound like – his laughter and his rapid-fire and witty repartee is hard to forget. I am reminded of his presence and his absence every single day. Whether it is a song heard on the radio, a facial expression on one of my grandson's dear little faces, or a mosquito.

As Henry Miller once said, the aim of life is to live, and to live means to be aware – joyously, drunkenly, serenely, divinely aware. I thank my boy for helping me live so fully – both when he was alive and now.

"Some people come into our lives and quickly go. Some people move our souls to dance. They awaken us to a new understanding with the passing whisper of their wisdom. Some people make the sky more beautiful to gaze upon. They stay in our lives for a while, leave footprints on our hearts, and we are never, ever the same."
-Flavia Weedn

About the Author
Christie McPhee

Christie leads a vibrant and love-filled life. The eldest of a family of five, Christie enjoyed a down-to-earth upbringing with ample amounts of home-made bread, a cottage on an island for summer-time adventures, a love of music, nature and adventure, and wholesome family values.

She moved from Ontario to Lions Bay, BC in 1988 with her then-husband and two sons. There she helped start the local café and was the editor of the village newspaper.

She now lives with her son, Sean, and his family, including two rambunctious little grandsons. For more than ten years, Christie has helped countless people learn how to reach and maintain their health goals and she practices what she preaches! In her sixties, Christie has more energy, vitality, and presence than she did when she was in her forties! Christie is known as a super-connector. She has a wide network of friends and has a knack for putting people together who would benefit from knowing each other (whether it's to fill a need for used furniture or a potential career opportunity). She loves to travel and enjoys exploring the history and culture of foreign countries. She is also a professional singer and has shared the stage with many fine musicians for over four decades. Most of her family members are very talented musicians and one of her great joys is singing with them. It is one of the ways she honours Duncan who was a very accomplished guitar player. Her spiritual practice has served her well for the last 20 years and it continues to be the beacon that helps her navigate her way through his loss to thriving in the present.

Is it time to make a change? Meet that challenge that's been holding you back?

Connect with Christie:

healthypresence@gmail.com

https://www.facebook.com/christie.mcphee1

CHAPTER FOUR

Warrior Heart

By Patricia Clum

It's hard to say the moment I fell in love with Bill, only that I knew there was no turning away from his steady gaze. A soul recognition perhaps with a deep knowledge of his lived life wisdom in his journey before we meet. My heart opened to the possibility of where our hearts and souls may take us.

So at this moment on the way to our fifth retreat of the year, as all was going wrong could go wrong, my heart softened witnessing him moving through another threshold of awareness. Before me, I witnessed my Warrior of Heart step into another inner battle of healing.

With more than ten years of travelling, city to city up and down the west coast of America, there is bound to be delays at borders and heavy traffic to slow down and change arrival times. All a perfect setup for building the pressure of bringing us both into the present moment.

He was taking deep breaths, moving through another layer of healing, in touch with a space within that was ready to let go. As I placed my hand over his heart, he became aware of the moment over 50 years ago, how vulnerable he felt as an 18-year-old young man walking through the gates of the prison. As he realized and then released the memory, breathed out the pain of the memory with each breath, his shoulders softened, his breath steadied. He settled and his whole being moved back into stillness. We were parked in the ferry lineup, knowing that all that was moving through us and what we were experiencing was preparing us for what was next.

We were only a couple of hours away from facilitating a live retreat with 14 beautiful souls. As I was holding Bill's hand, I knew that the depth of his experience that just passed through him was mirroring what was possible for each person sitting in a sacred circle for the next three days.

Bill wasn't always the man that could access his heart and stillness with breath, awareness, and devotion. Over the years as he has shared his story with me, as I have watched him support and literally hold another man while their hearts open during the retreat, I have been deeply moved by his incredible commitment to get to know himself, his courage, and his willingness to dive right in.

As I tell his story, understand these are my words of witnessing the man I love open to his god-self. This story is slices of his life, painting a picture of the road he has travelled. Some of you reading may know him differently, may have met him, or spent time with him in all his various experiences. Some of you may feel that you already know him or know a man very much like him. He is a man that through his life has turned his back to his yearning to know God and has tried everything possible to fight with and control his path to knowing himself. Each path he travelled the question always was echoing in and out of his awareness "Who am I"?

At 9 years old, he would run along the beaches in Florida, in the wonder of feeling and sometimes witnessing a translucent blue light following just behind him. The mere feeling of this brought him joy and excitement, yet not knowing what or why this mystery met with him off and on. It was around this time, he became quick at fighting fist to fist, to protect and defend himself. A warrior was born, passed down how to be a man, from father to son.

Being raised on a Military base was freedom at this young age, out from dawn to dusk, yet also had the dangers of being a boy and other boys testing your courage and strength. In his childhood, his family moved often from base to base and usually without much notice. His father, in the times he was home, would announce "Get your stuff packed - we are moving today". Bill remembers each time he sat in the back seat of the car with his brother and sister, looking out the back window, tears rolling down his cheeks as he waved goodbye once again to his friends.

From year to year and home to home, over time he decided it was too painful to love. As it was too painful to love, he became more focused on trying not to love.

He remembers coming home to his father and hearing both "Son, don't be too sad" and "Son, don't be too happy". His emotions and feelings began to be stuffed down, numbed out, and he developed an expression of being unapproachable. To some kids they admired his "coolness", to others they were afraid because with his attitude came his ability to box. His father would often turn him around and face the big kid that wanted to fight him. Over time Bill became known from base to base for his "one-punch knockout fights." He was lean and quick. It's this quickness that ended most fights before they really got started. His heart would beat fast, and he would internally pray that the fight would end quickly. The times he did get hit, he remembered, and promised himself he would be faster next time.

During these years he was brought up catholic and found the curiosity of God began to stir in his awareness. Soon the structure of the church began to challenge him. Although he was an altar boy and learned Latin for mass, when it was time to collect the wine and sacramental cookie, he always managed to have a few sips and sneak a bite or two. During the tithing time, he would sneak some coins for pinball at the community hall.

When his family moved to San Diego California he fell in love with surfing. The feel of the ocean, the stillness, the roar of the waves, the moment the broad glides towards the shore. Through the years, surfing always reminded him of his connection to self and the planet and became a devotion to him. The ocean became his mistress, every moment he could, he raced to spend time in the ocean.

Around this time, girls sparked his interest and he became curious and fascinated. Life was surfing, girls, school, and more fights. Soon school started being skipped... surfing and hanging out was more fun. Parties and rule-breaking added extra thrill and defiance for anyone trying to hold him back. The police would drive right on to the beach and wait for the ocean to bring Bill in so they could escort him back to school or the detention center for not going to school and blessing them with his attitude. It was at the beginning of the Vietnam war that Bill found himself standing in the courtroom before a frustrated judge. Bill's tan was dark, his raven hair neat, green eyes piercing, and standing strong, even though inside his mind he was screaming. It happened quickly, the hanging out and the breaking of rules, drinking, leading up to this moment with being charged in court for trying to sell marijuana to an undercover FBI agent.

"It's kids like you that are poisoning our country. You're almost 19-years-old. I am setting an example starting with you, of what we will not put up with. So, William Clum, I am sentencing you for 2 to 10 years to State Prison." The wind was knocked out of his lungs, he swayed in disbelief, yet stood strong and emotionless. As he was being walked to his cell, he thought his 18-year-old mind swirled with "How did this happen?' "How did I get here?"

Bill doesn't talk a lot about those years, only a few moments in time. He decided to get schooling and earned his aviation certifications, studying hard and trying to avoid trouble. He survived the prison riots and had the hard lessons of how friends become enemies and how enemies become friends. He learned that often those in power would take out their own pain on others, with force, humiliation and blame. His fighting skills and tenacity to push back saved his life emotionally and physically many times in prison. He worked out and became strong to defend and protect. Bill spent his 21st birthday in prison. On the bad days when he felt his mind was being lost, he would bang his head on the prison sink to stay sane. When surviving one of the harder realities of solitary confinement, Bill found himself on his knees praying and asking "Why?", he felt and heard, "You'll know in over 30 years."

At 23 years old with $24 in his pocket, his parents accepted him back into the family home. It was more challenging than he could have imagined, for even though he was free, he felt imprisoned within his soul. He quickly fell into drinking again, trying to chase away the echo of his prison time. One night as he was laying passed out in his bed, he woke up to his mother kneeling beside his bed with her face in her hands, tearfully praying to God that Bill find his way, and not be taken away from her again. He had never felt his mother so deeply, so heart broken and this moment cracked open Bill's heart, feeling his mother's love so deeply; with tears in his eyes, he promised would turn his life around.

Moving from aviation mechanics to the automotive industry, Bill began to build his business of an auto repair shop right in the heart of San Diego. Years passed, his business flourished, he continued to surf and found himself in love and with three children before his 30th birthday. With his successful auto repair shop, mentoring and leading 22 employees at one time, his life was full of family, adventures, and building his legacy. He was a firm and often tough boss, expecting the most from his employees and himself. Driven by the motivation of an anger and never ending desire to perform at the top of his league. He knew his humble beginnings and was going to show the world, and especially his father, that he had become successful and created wealth from determination and skill.

Behind closed doors, however, his internal struggle to know self kept him awake at night and searching. His religious commitment moved to Christianity through the young years of marriage and raising his three children. Through the decades his relationship to religion was changing and moving away from his Christian understanding which no longer nourished his soul, he began to lose focus of what fed his heart. His marriage suffered, and the stress of all the confusion and challenges in business with his personal choices added to his long road of divorce. His identity he had built was beginning to crumble and although his business was thriving, he was beginning to feel himself so very distant from the man he saw in the mirror every morning. Through this he stayed committed to providing for his children, juggle his business and also welcomed another child into his life.

He parented what he learned, adjusted as he could, always chasing the clock from one day to the next.

During these years, still pushing away love, he was introduced to cocaine in the late '80s and became a "functioning" addict. That addiction lasted for years until at one point the addiction controlled him.

It was his own children that, in their innocence and love for their father, ended up saving him from himself; the first time was in his realization through them that he was, in fact, an addict. On one particular day, in one particular moment, he became aware of the weight of his addiction and the impact on others and decided right at that moment to become clean and sober.

The next time his children, unknown to them, reinspired him to continue was while he was witnessing Tony Robbins on tv in the middle of the night. He realized that his own children were more emotionally mature than he was, and from that moment forward he made whatever choice was necessary to "grow up" and be the parent and father he yearned to be.

Bill's journey began to become ignited in a passion of getting to know who he was, not just a successful business owner, not just an addict, not just the mistakes of his past, his path opened to remembering who he was, truly. His warrior nature was stirred into a new territory of knowing himself and himself in relationship with others.

As his children became teenagers and into adulthood, he dove deeply into the waters of transformational work. Around this time, he was in top physical shape, but he noticed how winded he was climbing the stairs to go to his car after surfing for the day. Each step took all his wind and all his strength. At 55, he found himself lying on the surgery table for open-heart surgery repairing his mitral valve. The procedure went on for hours as his soul struggled and the complications during surgery had him on the edge of death and life. In the hospital, family and friends gathered, prayed and waited to see if he would come out of surgery safely. He came through, astounded by how his children and others supported him making it back into life. After being sent home, his healing days and nights were in his living room. With the extreme pain of ribs cracked and chest opened and the trauma of his heart healing, he sat and slept in a chair that could keep him upright so he could breathe and rest, balancing between pain and sleep. One evening as he was sitting in pain he started daring God to take him. Tears streaming down his cheeks, not knowing if he could survive even another day of the pain, he heard, "Before you decide, would you like to hear all those that prayed and will pray for you?" His chin dropped to his chest, surrendering to the moment and he said, "Okay". Within the next breath right before him in his living room, he witnessed the translucent blue cellophane dome embrace his whole being. His heart beat fast as he remembered this mystery visiting him as a child. Tears still flowing, he then heard thousands of voices praying, some he recognized, and some he knew he was yet to meet. This lasted extended minutes bringing in a depth of gratitude for life he had never experienced before. As he received the choir of voices in prayer, he whispered "I will stay, please take my life as I know it, and make my life in service to you, God."

As the years unfolded, from seminar to seminar, he began unwinding and discovering who he was underneath all his limiting ideas and beliefs of himself. Each road took him closer to who he always wanted to be, a man who embraced love, compassion, and vulnerability.

Bill and I met at a time after which we both had experienced years of transformation inquiry through seminars, spiritual retreats, of our own inner metamorphosis and willingness to always build a circle of support around us as we grew. We both were in a place within our own lives in which we knew what a relationship with another would create for our hearts. When we met, we knew our hearts would grow and finally our souls had a place of rest. That our next phase of life would move into creating our own legacy and meaning to what we will leave here on the planet after our last breath.

Within the first year of Bill and I meeting, we also met our mentor who would end up supporting both of us into becoming who we are today, for over ten years of the continual extraordinary adventure of the heart. Bill was turning 60 and I, 42 years old, both living in separate countries. We would travel back and forth learning to trust our time together and apart.

Charles, our mentor, would remind us over and over to let each other go as we grew. This internal letting go, broke through any old behaviours and expectations from any past experience. We also came to realize in a practical and everyday experience that it was up to us, individually and as a couple, to continue to nourish our relationship, our individual heart gifts awakenings, and our calling to bring our shared gifts to the planet. When I say "gift", the reference is because these "gifts" are usually such a surprise to self, that to begin to experience God-consciousness within for self is an extraordinary gift. Then to recognize that this gift is as unique and divine as your own fingerprint is the declaration to the universe that you are awakening to who you truly are and were always meant to be!

My gift flowed through me, unfiltered, unedited, messy, and unpredictable. In meeting Bill, the universe brought me the man that with simply his own presence, began to ground and give my "gift" space to land. When our mentor "kicked me out of the nest" to begin working with another, he simultaneously held Bill back. He held Bill back in such love, and compassion so Bill could truly recognize his own heart. Bill's deep devotion to know his god-self, walked him through profound thresholds of awakening. His "dark night of the soul" while moving through the threshold of loneliness changed his life. The months and years collided into a few weeks, he felt all there was to feel, all that he never had an opportunity to feel. Weeks of devoting to simple practices of heart: drinking water, walking, journaling, meditating, and allowing emotion to flow. Until one day he felt and experienced where at a soul level he believed he was separate from god-self. In the precise moment, that particular breath, the divine timing of his heart and soul, his organic healing of separation happened.

Bill and I have spent over 10 years offering the energy and holding for others in a group or individual setting. In the beginning, before the words were birthed and took form, we navigated through with instinct. Some moments were smooth and others awkward, innocently diving with the mysterious language of heart and soul. We made mistakes, and learned from them, recovered from them and grew from them. In our daily life and through each retreat we embraced the heart practices we encouraged to follow. We know that the practices are simple, yet within the simple comes the unwinding, comes the deeper listening and preserves the moment for self-awakening and life-changing realizations. We also know that the human mind tends to make everything that is live more complicated than it was ever meant to be, and if there is devotion to following one's own heart and listening to one's own soul, in the simple all is heard and felt. During one of these retreats, the impossible was being moved right before us. People's hearts were opening so deeply and profoundly, we fell to our knees in prayer, honour, and deep humility. In that magnetic wave of movement, the whole room fell into prayer. Praying for family, loved ones, humanity. Bill in his awe then heard in his heart, "These are the prayers you heard years ago, [after his open-heart surgery] they are now being answered, these voices, these souls."

To join Bill's path and be a part of Bill's healing of pushing away love and to witness and experience his gift in a constant state of growth and wonder is profound. He has become the love that he was always yearning for, he has stopped the internal war and laid down his sword, to have become the warrior of love that the world has been yearning. I am in humbled delight to witness other men follow in Bill's footsteps and learn to embrace their own hearts.

While Bill was in meditation at the beginning of our work together, out in the forest, taking in the fresh ocean air, he heard, "It's been thirty years. Would you like to know why you went to prison? I kept you in prison, safe from yourself, so you could be here with all these hearts."

I have had the pleasure of witnessing Men coming alive, breathing life into their own families and communities while trusting to stand in the fire with Bill. They lean into his wisdom, they lean into his unconditional love, they lean into the warrior that holds a lifetime of devotion in his heart. Most men, we have noticed, are tired of avoiding their own hearts, are awakening to their own feelings, are weary of their own inner struggles of awakening. When they stand before Bill, they experience his lived wisdom, some recognize right away that they are being welcomed home. Some do not quite understand, and their minds swirl with trying to figure out 'what just happened' when they meet Bill.

"You decide when you decide," Bill will share. It's the divine moment when soul and heart meet and there's no other way to go but in.

This story of Bill is for men that have always been looking for who they are, men that feel the yearning to truly know self. Men that love deeply, yet often don't know how to share. Men that are experiencing the echoes of the past as mistakes instead of lived wisdom awakening them into self. Men that are devoted to more, that often don't have words. Men that love humanity so deeply it hurts. Men that are looking for another man to lean into, another man to guide. Men that are waiting or playing still on the sidelines, as Bill would say, "Your time here is short; if this moment was your last breath, how would you spend it?"

For the women reading, we encourage you not to give up on men. Men hold so much more than often they are given credit for, more than often women can see. Women, as your voices arise, as your wisdom is birthed, as your hearts open, men feel you. Be the space for the willing man to be embraced. Women, men can be lost, yet men can also be the ones that hold the container of consciousness itself. The space between the stars.

Today we live in the ebb and flow of relationship, honouring our over 15 years of time together, sharing our lives with family and friends.

Our everyday life reflects our gifts; the work we offer is not separate from who we are.

The way we live and who we are organically moved into new beginnings, new fields, and new spaces of consciousness coming to move with and through us.

We stumbled into each other on a sunny Sunday spring day in San Diego so many years ago, introduced by a friend.

I knew the man beside me was a man that could ride the waves of change. I knew that we were brought together for something more powerful than I had words for at the moment. I felt his warrior of heart, I felt his wisdom, and most importantly he could feel my heart. I was felt and seen with delight through his eyes. Each day from that moment forward we share together the meeting in the spaces of heart and soul.

"Remember, all you are is already within you.
Your invitation is to know your own heart and soul in
your life time. How deep is your yes?!"

-Bill Clum

About the Author
Patricia Clum

Bill and Patricia Clum have been supporting others for over 10 years, providing spiritual guidance in the emotional and spiritual domain. Bringing awareness to hurts and emotions that are being revealed, supporting another through processes while facing and healing these fears. Embracing emotion, letting go of resistance, and living in the present moment, your divine nature is remembered. Self-acceptance with forgiveness heals and begins the transforming within your heart, living a life of fulfillment, and love.

Connect with Patricia:

Book your 20 min session; is your heart a yes?!

Join the community, sign up for an email, and receive two meditations to welcome your heart!

Website: www.evolutionoftheheart.com

Facebook Business Page: @evolutionoftheheart

Follow us on Instagram: @evolutionheart

CHAPTER FIVE

Goal: Get My Life Back!

By Jennifer Franklin

For most of my life, I've considered myself a fairly healthy person. Although my life started off tenuously, with my Mom very ill (a concerning birth), followed by several bouts of tonsillitis and painful earaches as a young child, then a tonsillectomy at age seven, things have gone fairly smoothly since then. My Mom teases me about how when I was a child, if I got a scratch, I'd be afraid it 'might bleed.' All of my life I have struggled with anything to do with needles. Like most people, I've had my share of adversities in my life, which I'm certain have made me a stronger person. I'm a pretty determined person when I'm on a path - once I get an idea in my mind, it becomes my focus.

I grew up in a close-knit family, in Vancouver, BC and we moved to White Rock, BC when I was twelve. I met my husband the year after I finished high school, and we've enjoyed 33 years of life's adventures together. We have two sons; one in his late teens, and one in his early twenties, and a lovely home beside a lake on Vancouver Island, BC. I have a job I enjoy as an Academic Advisor for a distance education centre, so I have the privilege of working from home.

The year I was turning 50 was going to be a fun year watching our two sons continue in their elite hockey pursuits, furthering our projects at our rustic off-grid cabin on the river, and looking forward to some adventures exploring new areas of Vancouver Island.

You don't know what you've got till it's gone

Out of the blue, I started having terrible stomach pains in the night, and about a month later I found my abdomen was blowing up like a balloon. I knew something was terribly wrong, but what was it?

Before long, I was short of breath, could barely walk 10 feet, and was sleeping sitting up just to be able to breathe. I was sent for loads of tests and scans which seemed to go on for weeks and were pointing toward some kind of cancer! At that point, I was just trying to survive and get through the day. Finally, during one of my several trips to the local emergency room, I got the diagnosis from one of the doctors that the markers were showing Lymphoma (a blood cancer) – a rare and aggressive one called Burkitt's.

On one of my visits to the emergency, while waiting for an appointment with the oncologist, and for a biopsy to be done, I was admitted to the hospital as things were progressing so quickly. It was then that I got the devastating news that I would need to leave home and go for treatment at Vancouver General Hospital (VGH) on the mainland (a five-hour trip) and that I should plan to be there from 4-6 months for treatment!

What? My mind was trying to comprehend how I was going to pick up and leave behind my husband, our boys, my work, and entire life, and just drop everything! How would this be possible? The doctors told me it would be a very difficult treatment to go through but that there was a very high chance of beating it. To put it mildly, I was terrified. It really came down to only one thing: *I had no choice.* If I was going to survive this, I was going to need the chemotherapy treatment urgently. There was no time to consider anything else.

While waiting to be admitted to VGH, there was another trip to Emergency where I ended up in ICU as my kidneys had shut down due to an overload of cells shed resulting from a drug that was supposed to reduce some of the fluid buildup. Once everything was stabilized, I was transported by ambulance to the ferry and directly to VGH. My dear Dad travelled over from another province to accompany me. I left my husband at home running the household and taking care of our boys and two dogs.

Once I got settled into the VGH Leukemia/Bone Marrow Transplant (BMT) unit (where they also treat Lymphoma), they got right to work performing minor surgery to insert a Hickman line so that all my bloodwork and chemo could go through this line rather than multiple needles every day. At that point, I knew I badly just wanted to get through this.

There was a small whiteboard on the wall beside my bed where I wrote: **GOAL: Get My Life Back!** I continued to look at this statement I had made as a reminder to myself and everyone else that I had a life to get back to and I was determined to get there.

I was prescribed a very aggressive mix of chemotherapy (CODOX/IVAC MacGrath protocol), to be done in four rounds, plus I needed eight different chemotherapy spinal injections. The chemotherapy successfully began shrinking the tumours after the first round. As I was able to get up and about more (and look in a mirror!), it became apparent that I had lost about 30 lbs and had quite a reduction of muscle mass. No wonder I felt so weak.

Because I'm originally from the Vancouver mainland, I was fortunate to have lots of family somewhat close to the hospital. I remember telling my brother that the doctors at VGH saved me once (when I was born) and that they were going to save me again!

My husband exhausted himself travelling back and forth on the ferry each week to stay for a few days with me to provide loving support and care, and lots of encouragement. Our sons, who were 15 and 18 at the time, were left at home to fend for themselves for part of the week – grocery shopping, making meals, feeding and playing with dogs, and going to school and work! I can't even imagine what they were going through.

My Dad stayed by my side much of the first two weeks of my stay at the hospital. He joked with me that he missed being there when I was born, as he was away working, and this was his way of making it up to me. After two weeks at the hospital, and one round of chemotherapy behind me, he felt I had stabilized, so he let me know he would head home again and that I was in good hands.

I was terrified of my Dad leaving. In fact, I felt such panic after he left that I started thinking about what I could do to stop the mounting anxiety. I decided to reach out to other family members to see if they would visit me. Thank goodness for my cell phone – my lifeline to the outside world. Being the planner and organizer I am, when I knew I was having a chemotherapy treatment scheduled, I 'booked' someone to come in for at least a couple of hours that day to be with me. I was really worried about feeling sick and not having anyone there. Having said that, the nurses and doctors were kind and attentive and highly trained to take care of patients in the Leukemia BMT unit. They also did their utmost to be sure I had the right drug to combat the ill effects of the chemotherapy. All of this went totally against how I usually live my life; I try to avoid prescription drugs if possible, and will look for natural ways to take care of my health. I was somewhat distressed that they were putting a lot of toxic chemicals into my body to combat my illness, but I did my best to push away these thoughts and focus on getting through the treatments. I also made use of the anti-anxiety medicines available when I had to go for a CT scan or a chemotherapy spinal. I felt that I needed to find a way to cope.

My husband and I were in touch several times a day through texts and calls. As well, I enjoyed being able to FaceTime with my husband and the kids, and have them show me around our home, 'see' our dogs, and look forward to what I had to return to.

I truly appreciated receiving text messages from family and friends checking in on me and giving me encouragement. Sometimes I was too exhausted to answer for a few days, but it was so nice to know I had someone to listen to me and boost me up.

Although I went to church when I was growing up, I don't actively attend now. I remember praying to God many nights in my hospital bed before going to sleep – I made him a deal that if I was allowed to live and continue my life, I would seek to help others.

I was in the hospital initially for just over three weeks, when suddenly I was told I would be released, and would become an outpatient for most of the other treatments. I couldn't believe it! What a scary moment – I was going to be away from having nurses and doctors right there to take care of things if something went wrong. I was accustomed to having my vitals checked twice a day, my bloodwork at early hours of the morning, and all my needs addressed. I tried to convince them to keep me longer and that I wasn't ready to leave. But they needed the bed for someone else and I would be moving somewhere, not sure where, to continue my outpatient treatment. There were places nearby I could rent, like a shared room at a lodge for cancer patients. I couldn't imagine getting myself back and forth to appointments at the hospital every few days, and how I would deal with moments when I didn't feel well or was unable to take care of myself.

Then it started to sink in what it would be like to be out of the hospital – freedom! I could eat the food I wanted, not have people waking me up early in the morning, and coming in and out all day poking and prodding. It would be quieter, and I could actually sleep. Hmm, this may not be such a bad thing after all.

I asked the nurse if I could get a wheelchair to get me out the door of the hospital. She told me unless I could walk out under my own power, I was not allowed to leave. I quickly made arrangements with my two Aunts – my Mom's younger sisters – to pick me up. They knew I would have trouble walking out as I was still very weak, so they were prepared to carry all my 'stuff' and hold me up, one on each side, so I could leave. I think one Aunt joked in a text to me that they were on their way to help me escape!

Although I have a very close relationship with my Aunts, I felt very awkward asking them if they would be willing to have me stay with them – both live about 45 minutes from the hospital and one doesn't drive. I guessed that maybe I would stay with them for a couple of weeks while I got my strength back and then I could move into one of the lodges. I was so grateful that I was able to stay with my Aunt the entire 3-1/2 months! Since she was already doing so much for me (groceries, meals, laundry, calling the hospital in the middle of the night to ask what to do about a persistent high fever), I tried to arrange all my rides with other family members.

The outpatient visits were exhausting. My husband or a family member drove me to the Leukemia BMT *daycare* unit, which is part of the hospital, where my bloodwork and vitals were checked, I would see a Doctor, sometimes be given a blood transfusion if needed or be booked for chemotherapy treatment. Two times I had to be admitted back into the hospital for chemotherapy treatments that required round-the-clock observation. My husband on his visits was so encouraging, telling me 'we logged another day'; getting closer to being done the treatments. We had many hard conversations and tears along the way, but you really see what someone is made of when you go through this kind of adversity. All of it confirmed what a solid, caring, loving husband I have!

On one of my visits to the daycare unit, my sister-in-law was with me and we were sitting there chatting about things, and I was telling her how my relationship with my Dad had become so much closer and she termed it: *Gifts in the Garbage*! This totally sums up so many things that are terrible or traumatic events that we gain 'gifts' from. I guess some people would call that the silver lining.

I finally got through all of my treatments after 4 months and was allowed to return home. What an exciting and terrifying day. I worried about being far away from the Doctors who had been taking care of me, just in case something went wrong.

Life back at home was wonderful and stressful too. So many changes in our lives and being home was awkward for a while until we got into a new routine. While I was recovering, I realized that I needed to stop viewing myself as ill in order to be on a path to wellness.

Six months after my initial diagnosis, I went for a PET scan and received the happy news that there was no evidence of any residual Lymphoma. I continued on with monthly bloodwork and I see a naturopath regularly who has been helping me eat in a way that doesn't overburden my body, plus I use immune-boosting supplements and anti-cancer type supplements. Even two years later, I still have a lower White Blood Cell count than a normal person so I continue to do everything I can to boost this.

I fulfilled my goal and GOT MY LIFE BACK! I have been able to get back to all my regular activities, and I feel strong and healthy.

Being so close to having lost my life gives me an entirely different perspective when I wake up in the morning. No matter what, I am so glad and grateful to be here. I realize how close I came to missing out on the rest of my life.

How I Got Through

Some of the attributes I used to get through this adversity in my life are my determination, stubbornness, and hopefulness.

My primary external resource was for sure my husband and my family. My road to wellness would have been much more challenging without the support I had from the people closest to me. All my life, my Mom has always encouraged me to believe in myself and that I could do anything I set my mind to.

Mindset is at the forefront of overcoming any adversity. Overcoming adversities whether they are small or large, helps to flex your mental toughness muscles. Getting past hard times and hurdles shows you that you can do it! My step-mom, who has battled through some serious health challenges, told me I needed to get angry and be determined to fight like I've never fought before, and to convince myself that I could beat this! You need to be willing to fight for what you want in your life. Everything worth fighting for is usually a hard road, but the end result is worth it.

I was very fortunate that the company I work for was so supportive and allowed me the time I needed, to get well.

Here are my 5 tips for choosing success over adversity:

- ❖ Ask for help from a professional
- ❖ Ask for help from family and friends
- ❖ Believe that your body is resilient
- ❖ Believe that you have the mental toughness it takes to reach your goal or overcome your adversity

❖ Have a complete focus on your end goal and where you are headed

Going through this illness and getting well again shows me anything is possible.

Take nothing for granted. Be grateful for all the wonderful people you have in your life.

Stay focused on your goal. Think about what you will have when you overcome your adversity.

About the Author
Jennifer Franklin

Jennifer continues to enjoy life on beautiful Vancouver Island in BC, Canada with her husband and two dogs. She and her husband are enjoying rediscovering the things they love to do while they are semi-empty nesters with their sons often away from home with university courses, hockey, and work.

Jennifer has enjoyed many years working as an Academic Advisor for a distance education centre. Previously she has worked for various software companies and always enjoyed her customer service and administrative roles. Jennifer has always had a dream of helping other people fulfill their health and wellness goals. She has a strong interest and personal experience with alternative therapies, holistic healing, and nutritional health.

She invites you to visit her Holistic Living Health website where she regularly shares information and tips on health and wellness-related subjects, to inspire you to live your best life every day.

Connect with Jennifer:

www.holisticlivinghealth.com

CHAPTER SIX

Brilliant Love

By Diane Paull

I am grateful for my gratitude practice. I am grateful for a warm place to live, enough quality food to eat and great friends and family. It wasn't always like this. Three years ago I was homeless, reeling from the trial of our beautiful daughter Rosie's murder and in lots of pain.

I look forward to the next step in my transition. I have finished treatment for Non-Hodgkins Lymphoma. Both of my biological adult children were in bad accidents in December 2018, my stepdaughter Rosie was murdered in 2015, her Dad, my late husband, Arthur died in 2011. My Mother died in 2012, and my Dad in 2018 while I was receiving chemotherapy treatments.

I still have difficulty finding the right words.

I am so blessed to have family and friends show up to care for me.

My pals in the building keep me laughing and make sure I have rides and meals. I have found home and my circle continues to grow.

It wasn't always that way.

Being with Arthur and our blended families gave me more skills to navigate this new chapter. How he set his priorities helped me carry on by keeping those traditions alive. Creator first, myself, family and then community. In keeping with the life Arthur and I created for ourselves, I focused on what I was able to do and that led me to spend Mom's last month together in Manitoba.

We all became homeless/underhoused with Arthur's death. Thankfully, the Women's Centre helped me find housing in a building built by the local Legion. Unfortunately, no guests for more than 3 days, so one Son arrived on my doorstep, needing housing, just before another Son arrived to notify me that Rosie had been identified by her tattoo ...

Our world fell apart. Moved out of my safe senior housing to an adorable old house out of town with Son to help each other through this tragedy. Ten days after we moved into our new place he ended up in hospital on suicide watch ... and I ended up homeless ... again.

During the 2 years before Rosie's murder trial, I managed to find a couple of caregiving and gardening jobs that came with beautiful rooms. When the murder trial began three years ago, I was in so much pain I could hardly eat. I thought the lack of appetite and stomach pains were my diverticular disease flaring up from the stress of being homeless and dealing with grief. I was feeling quite tired and wasn't sure I could keep up my work schedule. Lucky for me, between the end of the trial and sentencing, a suite became available in the same seniors' building, and I was able to move back into safe, secure, affordable housing again. Just in time as I was diagnosed with Non-Hodgkins Lymphoma and cancer treatment began quite soon thereafter.

A month later, I woke up crying for Rosie knowing that if she was here she would help me navigate the Cancer Journey, and care for me. My dear Granddaughter - Rosie's oldest daughter - contacted me as soon as she woke up, asking if I was ok and did I need anything as she had a nightmare about me. Our beautiful friend Karen showed up and stayed with me while I challenged the medical system, trying to decide what was the best plan of action, took me to my appointments and stayed to take care of me while I completed therapy. I cried out to Arthur for help ... he sent his Native American Church people who happened to be connected to our dear friend Karen. A Navaho Elder was visiting and was able to be in ceremony with us for a Crystal Gazing Ceremony. It revealed the trauma throughout my life that contributed to this disease. The next NAC Ceremony revealed that I needed chemotherapy.

Rosie's five daughters have been very helpful and visited often while I was housebound. The joy I felt with our blended family filled my spirit.

We build resilience together.

Resources, discipline, courage, resilience, external resources, family, community.

After chemotherapy, I participated in a study from UBC Nursing School to rewire my brain to manage pain.

Here are my 5 tips for choosing success over adversity:

- ❖ Gratitude Attitude
- ❖ Prayer
- ❖ Healthy food
- ❖ Time with family and friends
- ❖ Activities with joy

People want to help. Let them. That gave me the strength to keep going. Couch surfing with family, changing places every week or less, so as not to wear out my welcome … is how I've lived for periods of homelessness.

Ten years ago, the Spirits came to us and Arthur let me know that this would be our last Christmas together. Nine years ago, the year Arthur left us and during the last month in our home on Indian Land, I let our community support me in building a drum from his last Elk, to sustain me while I learned to navigate this new life without his spiritual leadership. I am so blessed our family and friends show up when I often don't even know I need help.

I am discovering what this next chapter will be.

Rosie's girls have been very helpful and visited often while I was housebound, and often came by to help with our youngest grandchild. Having our blended family playing together was the best therapy and I felt like we were building resilience together.

Five years have passed since our Rosie was murdered in the most horrific fashion. Her girls have blossomed into fine young women. They recently put together a luncheon to celebrate her youngest grandchild and hosted a family potluck later that day. Keeping up their Mother's traditions ... she would be very proud.

Our blended Family of Children, Grandchildren and Great Grandchildren are wonderful gifts.

During the darkest of times, I read and listen to spiritual music, Louise Hay, Sara Raymond, Dee Doherty. And I have learned to ask for help. I have learned the power of prayer. It is my daily practice. When I am stressed, I pray to the Holy Spirit for at least seven minutes.

Be kind generous and peaceful.

Thank you, Arthur, for choosing me and bringing me a Bonus Family.

About the Author
Diane Paull

Diane Paull has adventured in many home-based businesses including Secretarial, Catering, and newspaper support while raising two children on her own. She began facilitating workshops for the YWCA in 1981 and assisted with the Excellence Series in the 1990s. When her youngest graduated from high school she became a certified scuba diver and travelled up the Inside Passage.

Diane received a Diploma of Excellence in Life Skills Coaching and accepted a job at Sto:lo Nation. There she met the man of her dreams, Arthur Paull, and together they formed Kw'i:tsel Consultants, Adventures in Self Development.

During a beautiful backyard wedding, they became a blended family.

Moving company administration, office manager for Seeing Without Glasses, HIPPY Home Visitor, Women's Resource Centre, and her own Ms. Friday office support services business kept Diane busy until closing the doors to nurse Arthur until he passed.

CHAPTER SEVEN

A Mission to Advance Women in the Workplace

By Maureen McKinnon

I have been an entrepreneur since I was 25 years old. I'm a natural leader, as I like to tell people what to do... or so my family tells me. Coming from a family of entrepreneurs, my parents didn't freak out but rather supported me in my ventures.

As a serial entrepreneur, my businesses have included executive leadership coaching, business consulting, training, real estate, insurance, and recruitment.

All of my businesses have been based on helping people have better lives. I am a teacher, mentor, coach, cheerleader, and genuinely care for and really like people.

I have a Masters of Science in Management, a Masters of Science in Financial Services, Certified Executive Coach, Certified

Business Coach, and have been an instructor with Langara College Continuing Studies.

I enjoy CFL football, BC Lions games, reading, networking, social events, dancing, travel, spending time with family and friends, and fun!

How it All Started

I have been supporting women's empowerment for the past 20 years in both my work and personally through volunteering.

Twenty years ago, my friend and business partner, Donna Ramsden and I started a Recruiting Company – we assisted candidates to land a new job with employers looking to fill roles in their companies. We successfully placed 150 people per year in new positions.

Close employer working relationships have given me insight into hiring and promotion decision making. This knowledge has been instrumental in my work as a Career Coach and Executive Leadership Coach.

Once our new recruiting company had been operating for about nine months, Donna and I decided that we should volunteer with a business organization.

Our decision making proceeded along the lines of since our office is in downtown Vancouver on Howe Street, we should join the Vancouver Board of Trade (VBOT). So, we did.

Shortly after, I was asked to volunteer on one of the board's committees. The committee that intrigued me most was the new Leaders of Tomorrow Mentorship Program.

The Leaders of Tomorrow (LOT) Mentorship Program gives students the opportunity to learn from leading industry professionals through business mentors, a program of LOT events, VBOT events, and volunteering in the community. It provides a bridge from the academic world of studies into the real-life "working" world.

I had just missed the opportunity to be a Business Mentor matched to one of the students, so they asked me to join the Executive Board for the LOT. I was absolutely thrilled to be involved with such a great group of business mentors, enthusiastic students, fabulous Program Manager – Rebecca Clapperton (kudos to Rebecca for her great work) and dedicated board staff.

I flung myself wholeheartedly into the LOT program, spending 10 – 12 hours a week at the board working with the LOT program or attending board events. I was talking to everyone so much about the fabulous LOT program that my Mom asked me if I was "in a cult".

I was enormously proud to be asked to be the third Chair of the LOT program during 2003 – 2004. All in all, I was involved with the Leaders of Tomorrow Mentorship Program for seven years.

During my term as Chair, I was asked to submit my name to be a Director at the Vancouver Board of Trade. I was successfully nominated to the board. I am immensely proud of my time as a Director at VBOT, from 2003 thru 2006. The board work was extremely satisfying; it was great to be a part of a senior business group that works hard to lead, unite, and champion business, serve their members, and to ensure the region's business community thrives.

I enjoyed my volunteer roles so much at the VBOT that in the ensuing years I have been involved with over 12 women's groups in the Lower Mainland, BC. I have been a member, event participant, volunteer, committee member, board member, mentor, coach, panellist, and speaker. The groups include WXN, WTC, PWN, WEF, YWIB, CCW, Lean in Canada, FWE, VanWIT, WTCBC, WWS, WIL, and WEC.

Volunteering has enhanced my life. I've met thousands of great people, attended hundreds of fabulous events, had many wonderful experiences, and been inspired regularly. Now, it never occurs to me not to volunteer.

Currently, I am the Co-Chair Vancouver Chapter for Women in Leadership Foundation (WIL) and on the National Advisory Committee for Women's Economic Council (WEC).

I am a passionate advocate for empowering women to reach their full potential. I live and breathe helping women to advance in their careers and life. I proudly walk my talk!

My CFL Journey

One of my most unique experiences ever was in the summer of 2004. I was the Chair of the LOT program and a Director at the VBOT and was invited to sit at the head table for a VBOT event. The event was the Kickoff Luncheon for the BC Lions CFL Football Season and the head table was located on the 50-yard line at BC Place.

Sitting at the table was the legendary General Manager: Bobby Ackles, the winningest coach of the league: Wally Buono, the Vice President: George Chayka, industry leaders: Dennis Skulsky, Tom Malone, Bill Wildeman, Moray Keith, and me.

Having grown up with four sports-loving brothers I knew who Bobby and Wally were. I was thinking to myself about how jealous all my brothers would be when I tell them.

During the luncheon, the table started talking about the BC Lions Waterboys. So, I asked, "Who are the Waterboys? Turned out I was sitting with the founders. The Waterboys are a group of business leaders who act as team ambassadors; it was created by Bobby to re-establish the passion and aura surrounding the Lions and engaging with the community.

So, I asked, are there only men in the group? They said that they have one woman, Jamesie Bower. I then asked if I could join. They said that they would be thrilled to have me join and that's how I became the second woman Waterboy!

In 2011, Vancouver was awarded the 99th Grey Cup Festival, and I asked Scott Ackles, the General Manager of the Festival, if I could volunteer on the committee. He passed my name to the Director of Volunteer Workforce, Christine Nicholls, and that's how I became the Chair of the Volunteer Orientation & Training committee responsible for training the 700 volunteers - another fabulous experience. My brothers are so proud of me.

When Vancouver was awarded the 102nd Grey Cup Festival in 2014, I was asked if I would come back and Chair the Volunteer Orientation & Training committee. I said I'd be delighted to be involved again.

In addition to the Grey Cup Festivals, I have volunteered with the BC Junior Football Association, been a Director with Langley Rams Junior Team and with CFL initiatives.

I continue to be a proud active member of the BC Lions Waterboy, and a passionate BC Lions, and CFL football fan. Ask me how many football games I've attended!

It's amazing the things that can happen in your life – if you just ask!

The Day That Changed My Life

Friday, Oct. 24th, 2014: BC Economic Forum: *Women as a Catalyst for Growth*

I was excited to attend this event, the first of its kind in Vancouver. A working committee representing over 25 different women's business networks came together to create this event. Over 400 community and government leaders and influencers from across the province came together. I was considered one of the influencers – imagine that.

The Catalyst Research Report demonstrated the impact of women leaders as a catalyst for growth and profitability. According to Catalyst's Bottom Line study, "companies with more women board directors outperform those with the fewest by 66 percent return on invested capital, 53 percent return on equity and 42 percent return on sales".

The Report revealing the following statistics:

Women make up 47 percent of the Canadian labour force. The 2014 Catalyst Census shows that women account:

CEOs	5.3 %
Board Members	15.3%
Senior Officers	18.1%
Management Positions	35%

These statistics were, to me, the most startling of the day. I was horrified and almost in tears as I realized the stark reality: we, as women, had not moved the gender equity in leadership very far in the last fifteen+ years. I was disturbed by these facts over the weekend and they affected me for days and weeks following the event.

I decided to commit to myself and my work to helping women advance their careers. It changed my life direction!

My Mission

My mission is to help women balance gender equity in leadership roles. This is my legacy.

The UN Secretary-General, Mr. Antonio Guterres, has stated that achieving gender equality and empowering women and girls is the unfinished business of our time, and the greatest human rights challenge in our world.

At the rate we're moving forward it is estimated we will reach balanced leadership in 2227. We can't wait that long!

Since 2015, I have focused on working with talented women to advance their careers: gain new responsibilities, lead projects, lead teams, find and use their voices, seize leadership opportunities, gain promotions, and land new jobs.

More recently, starting in 2019, my work has shifted to a laser focus on getting more talented women promoted into management, leadership, and senior leadership roles.

Pivoting My Business

I decided to pivot my company from working with entrepreneurs to working with talented ambitious professional women to reach their full potential and advance their careers and lives.

How was I going to make that commitment happen?

During the rest of 2014 and early 2015, researching the subject became my new "job". I focused on identifying the barriers to women's advancement which caused the issues and challenges women face in the workplace.

The research provided three barriers to focus on:

1. Lack of Sponsorship, Advocacy, Champions, and Role Models

2. Less access to Critical Roles and Experience

3. Self-limiting Mindset including:

Feeling like a fraud, imposter syndrome, second-guessing your decisions, dismissing your achievements, underestimating your skillset, not accepting compliments, and lack of confidence.

The place to start was with the self-limiting mindset. From my own experience talking with hundreds of talented women, it breaks my heart to meet so many women who don't "see" the talented professional that I "see" when talking with them. It doesn't seem to matter what role level or years of experience they have.

They need help to transform the self-limiting mindset into what I coined "talent mindset." My definition of a Talent Mindset is the absolute belief (deep in your bones) in yourself, your talents, the value you bring and the results you deliver. Building rock-solid confidence in yourself is the cornerstone of career advancement.

It all starts with you.

Talent Mindset

The goal was to build a process working with women that would achieve the results of building rock-solid confidence. Working with over 100 women in the next three years, we discovered the practical action steps to acquire a talent mindset and successfully achieve their career goals.

When you acquire your Talent Mindset, magical things happen:

- ❖ Kyla got a job interview for a job she never applied for but wanted. After the interview process, she determined the job wasn't the role she wanted.

- ❖ Vicky took control of her interviews and started interviewing the employers to make sure the job would fit what she wanted.

- ❖ Helen saw a job posting that was written for her and she applied with a tailored resume and cover letter, she got the job, promotion, and a salary increase of 18%.

- ❖ Sarah negotiated a higher salary, a signing bonus, and more vacation time before starting her new role as a Senior Account Manager.

- ❖ Amelia created a tech presentation for a project that she was team manager on that was delivered at a conference in the spring of 2020. The virtual presentation was a Case Study using the conference sponsor's software. The sponsor liked the presentation so much they asked her if they could use it and they would acknowledge her in their global marketing campaign.

The transformation results are amazing from past clients. The talented women "see" their talented selves.

"You've opened my eyes to a whole new world of possibilities and have given me the confidence to believe the sky is the limit."
-Helen

The 4 Steps to Acquire a Talent Mindset

1. Discover Your Unique Strengths — Your Competitive Advantage

Start with making a list of your work skills:

a) Things you are good at

b) Things others say you're good at

You should find some duplicate skills listed on both lists (a) and list (b).

2. Expand Your Understanding of Your Skill Set

Select 3 skills that are the most relevant for your current role. Create stories from examples of using your skillset where you were successful.

My suggested framework is to start with the situation/problem before, describe your actions and the positive result. Remember, you are the Hero in your story.

3. Start Your Success Journal — Gather Social Proof of your Accomplishments.

Gather in one place your resume, job description, performance review, portfolio, documents, photos, emails from colleagues, superiors, clients recognizing your great work, awards, certifications, degrees, articles, press releases, etc.

When you review all this 3rd party acknowledgement of your talents, you will "see" and believe the talented professional you are.

4. Create Your Value Proposition Statement

Describe the value you bring explained in business results, why you do what you do, how you do it differently and better than others.

You'll stand out as your presence shifts, be more confident, smile more, be more positive and optimistic, speak out more, not be afraid to be heard, share your achievements, and share your ideas. You'll promote yourself and your results to the decision-makers in your organization.

My client, Marie, has had the most dramatic results:

"Our journey has allowed me to gain my talented leader mindset, boost my confidence, increase self-awareness, "Find my Voice", learn how to promote myself, my team and my results, increase engagement of my team, create & maintain strategic relationships and elevate my executive presence.

Three promotions later, my salary and total compensation have increased from $60,000 annually as a team lead to $125,000 as a Director of Vancouver Operations in a global company."

It is possible for you, as a talented woman, to gain your desired career goals! Let's make it happen for you, too.

Join me in my journey; let's keep moving forward to balance leadership gender equity. You too can help!

Three Things You Can Do to Support Women Career Advancement

- ❖ Commit to mentoring a promising young female leader.

- ❖ Nominate your female colleagues and women you admire for awards and recognition for their contributions.

- ❖ Engage in continuing the conversation with friends, family, colleagues, and especially with men to change the work environment, adding more diversity and inclusion and promoting more women in leadership roles.

We can make a difference!

About the Author
Maureen McKinnon

Maureen McKinnon's mission is to help more women gain leadership roles to balance gender equity in corporate leadership. She helps talented women get promoted and make more money!

Maureen has an impressive ability to make the women around her feel encouraged, confident and proud of themselves. She is a consummate professional. Her experience, wealth of knowledge, and business 'savvy" are clearly evident in the first few minutes of meeting her.

As a serial entrepreneur, she has a diverse professional career spanning executive leadership coaching, business consulting and development, training, real estate, insurance, and recruitment.

Her role as Executive Leadership Coach supports leaders/managers to maximize their unique leadership capabilities, grow their strengths, develop their people management skills, enhance their executive presence, and get promoted.

As a women's advocate, she is passionate about championing future women leaders. Maureen has been a member, participant, speaker, and/or volunteer for over 15 years with 12 different women organizations. Currently, she is the Women in Leadership Foundation's Vancouver Chapter Co-Chair and a member of the National Advisory Committee for the Women's Economic Council.

Maureen holds a Masters of Science in Management and a Masters of Science in Financial Services. She is a Certified Executive Coach and Certified Business Coach. She has been an instructor with Langara College Continuing Studies.

She enjoys CFL football, BC Lions games, reading, networking, social events, dancing, travel, spending time with family and friends, and FUN!

Connect with Maureen:

If you would like to learn more, visit www.mckcareer.com.

CHAPTER EIGHT

Falling Into the Light

By Carolina Parker

A typical day in my life could start with a jog in the Royal Botanic Garden in Sydney, Australia or a walk through the colourful streets of Mong Kok's flower market in Hong Kong. Working as an International flight attendant, the global village becomes your playground. One day I could be meeting a friend for a West End show in London and the next I could be walking my dog under a canopy of giant cedars in the coastal mountains of British Columbia, where I call home. My supportive husband and two freckle-faced ginger children are there to greet me with joy and hugs when I arrive home, along with our rescue cat and dog, at their feet.

My husband and I consciously built this life, as raising children was important to both of us. With each of us being avid backpackers, continuing to travel was also a priority. We began dating in 1994 while backpacking in Guatemala and always planned to continue experiencing the world this way with our children.

None of it has come easy, we worked hard and sacrificed, missing out on events back home to work and save to achieve our travelers' way of life. I refer to it as a champagne lifestyle on a beer budget.

At the age of seven, my family left my birthplace, Montreal, to move to Newfoundland, where my dad had secured a job at the university. During the late 70's rise of Quebec sepa-ratism, my entire family left Montreal and spread across North America. After completing grade two at a private school in St. Johns, our family - including both a fish tank and an unruly Irish Setter - left Newfoundland in an orange Volkswagen Westy to drive across the country and rejoin our extended family in Vancouver.

I grew up with my two sisters, my grandparents, and surrounded by cousins, aunts, and uncles, all very close and socially tight; friends in high school, romanticized about how close my family was, and how nice things like our Friday night Ambleside beach barbeque tradition was. I grew up surrounded by full houses, tables covered in tasty food, loud laughter, and plenty of love.

That's not to say that life didn't have its challenges; it did. After arriving in Vancouver for grade two, we moved six more times before I started high school. Life out West was more costly than Montreal and Newfoundland, so my mum had to work.

The family's social time became boozier and alcoholism started to affect my family, which led to my parents' separation and general family turmoil. I left home and flew overseas at eighteen.

My new life on the road excited me, I was eager for new experiences and I couldn't get enough. For the next decade or more, I didn't actually stay in one place for more than six months at a time until my husband and I bought our first home and started our family.

Motherhood had me in my element. We were living in a diverse neighbourhood in a one-hundred-year-old character house on what felt like Sesame Street. I was with a man I loved and two beautiful children and I was happy.

Near the end of my second maternity leave, I treated myself to a Rolfing program before returning to work full time. Rolfing is a form of deep tissue massage of the muscles and fascia. My Rolfing program consisted of a two-hour massage per week, in conjunction with a body awareness class. It was unlike any massage, acupuncture, or chiropractor work that I had ever done, as Rolfing is not about passively receiving treatment, but also learning about each part of our body and its movement, corresponding to the massage session. The idea is treating the issue at the root; when facia is evenly spaced throughout your body all will fall into place as it should.

Many people in the group shared their experiences during these exercises we discovered together. Most were there because they suffered some sort of chronic pain or had trauma, which had manifested in a physical form. I suffered from chronic lower back issues and tension between my shoulder blades. I had always been naturally athletic but couldn't place any injury to the pain, yet had written it off as a sports injury. The nagging pain interfered with life so much that one year at the school Christmas concert my daughter was handed the mike on stage and asked her holiday wish, she replied, "I want Santa to bring my mummy a new back".

During one of the massage sessions, while I lay breathing deeply, my mind began to flash through scenes of a dream. In these flashes, I was in a bedroom and someone else was there. It was not my bedroom, and the only thing I could recognize was a pink stuffy dog that I had as a child. I was there, and there was also a man. Nothing was in focus, but something very wrong was happening. I then remembered walking home afterward, and I was concentrating on my feet and my flip-flops as I walked.

An overwhelming feeling instantly washed over me. That room belonged to the man who had given me that stuffed dog, the same man who was there with me in my dream. I knew the man to be a friend of my father's during the heavy drinking years. When I got home, I told my husband, "I think I was abused as a child".

Andrew, my husband, held me. I told him about this man and the little that I knew about him. All I really knew is he had been a drinking buddy of my Dad. I remembered that my mum really did not like him and that he drove a van with dark windows and that he was in our life when I was about eight or nine years old.

That was the only memory flash I had during the Rolfing program. My Rolfing practitioner was also the person who told me that I needed to allow myself to believe that I could experience life without my chronic back pain. I needed to allow myself to actually visualize my living without pain.

One night in movement class, I realized that my bad posture and concaved chest were due to an attempt to protect my heart by sinking it into a sheltering pose, essentially hiding it. Barry the instructor was discussing this and I felt like he was speaking directly to me as though he spoke about this trait directly for my benefit.

It was a long time that I held this knowing inside me, just held it without further exploration. Life was full at the time and there wasn't a window for me to be introspective. The elephant was there though, in the background, kind of stabbing me over and over, similar to the feeling of chronic back pain. It is always there lingering, keeping me aware of its presence, holding me on edge of the abyss. I walked around as a conscious observer of myself, noticing my posture and how my head led me forward as I walked. I worked on trying to lead instead with my heart. If you were to draw lines, spreading out from my throat to my sides, and then across my chest, this triangle would designate the heart space. I would push forward and try to lead myself from there, rather than push forward from my head. I also noticed how often I clenched my hands into fists with my thumbs tucked in. When I noticed myself clenching, I stretched my hands and walked with them held upward and open to receive, which was something I had learned in yoga.

Around this time, we sold our house in the city and moved to a small coastal town forty-five minutes away from Vancouver, by ferry ride. It wasn't until we had really settled into our new life there that I began to allow myself time to really think about all of this. That is a bit of a lie, it wasn't that I had control and was choosing to delve into remembrance. The truth is, it forced itself back into my thoughts and wouldn't stand down. I had suffered through depression in adolescence and recognized this same darkness as it returned to me and took control of my thoughts. The voice inside my head was no longer an encouraging ally, but a dark force haunting me, pushing me to go deeper into the darkness.

I did some research and discovered that there were methods that I could use to help recall memories, like hypnotherapy and such. I learned that I might not have success if the memories were from a very early age and a full understanding of the events had not been formed at the time, but I made a silent declaration to do my best to uncover my truth.

I rarely went to see my doctor so when I went, I always had more than one thing to address and had to prioritize. When I next went to my doctor it was for sleeping pills and compression nylons for work, but instead, I found myself blurting out all of my stories, with my unsuspecting doctor listening as I sobbed. Not once did this incredible man look at his watch or waver in the slightest in his undivided attention on me. He asked me a few questions, took a few notes, and we just sat together. I will forever be grateful for his caring words that he shared with me at this most vulnerable time. He told me that I was brave. He shared stories with me and even made me laugh. He told me that I was strong to have built the family that I had and to have the relationship with my husband that I have. He shared stories of others he knew that had experienced sexual abuse and told me about the sad lives and situations they found themselves in. He made me feel proud of the person that I had become. By the time I left his small office with his referral in my hand, the tiny waiting room was jam-packed with patients, and all the eyes were on me and my puffy, tear-soaked face. I was sure that they had heard it all, I muttered sorry and left quickly.

From there the unravelling journey began.

Shortly after that, I remember being with my son, we had just picked my daughter up from a play date at a new friend's house on a farm. We had parked outside of the gate, at the roadside away from the house, and when we left, my car wouldn't start due to a dead battery. This wasn't a big deal and had been in this situation more than once, but at that moment there was no reasoning with my brain about any of that. I was in a full blown anxiety attack, right there with my young children. I could have simply walked back to ask the nice people for a jump start but I was so overwhelmingly debilitated, I could only panic. These types of anxiety attacks became so frequent that day to activities became a new challenge for me to overcome. I had to take a leave from work as I could no longer trust my ability to deal with an emergency situation if required to do so during a flight.

I started to see a therapist regularly, where I learned that once my memories came back they could show up randomly, which they did, with little warning, and rarely at a time when I could deal with them.

One day that stands out for my husband, was him coming home for lunch to find me crying uncontrollably, curled up on the couch, while a pile of kids were playing on the trampoline in the back yard. Andrew tried so hard to say the right thing and to support me, but he too was scared at the sight of his strong, stable wife crumbling in front of his eyes. I wasn't able to share the memories that were showing up in my head with him, I couldn't bear to have to hold him through the pain I was suffering.

I had to process the memories as they came. I needed so badly to weep for that little girl who had remained stoic. I had held on to these tears long enough. It was hard, some days I would have a little too much wine to shut off my thoughts. Some days the idea of getting out of bed was too daunting so wallowing safely in the darkness was where I stayed, covers up to my chin. My husband held our life together during those periods, cooking nice dinners, and keeping the kids active and entertained. Behind the scenes, we were flailing, trying to navigate each day. I felt as though someone had pulled the rug from underneath me, I was kicking my legs, attempting to find a ground that no longer existed.

At lunch one day in the city, I shared what I had been going through with an old friend. She grilled me on my memories and told me that my sex life was too normal and that I would be more fucked up than I am if it were true, and she just wasn't sure it really happened.

I went to my mother for more information. I could remember her not liking this particular guy. My dad didn't really bring new friends home often, and I didn't remember how they had become friends. Mum couldn't remember his full name. I used to go to Stardust roller skating rink with my Dad and him. Stardust had a bar. I would roller skate, I loved rollerskating, it was so much fun. I could skate backwards and swerve back and forth. I especially loved the loud music.

I used to have a reoccurring dream throughout my teens and maybe even my twenties. I was leaning on the outer edge of a skating rink; I was maybe nine or ten in the dream. The lights were dimmed and strobes bounced on the rink, ceiling and walls. I watch the big kids skating hand in hand, round and round the rink. There were a few variations of this dream, and in another version, the big kids raced each other holding brooms sticks with horse heads between their legs, the music playing into this horse racing theme.

In the eighties, I used to go to Stardust with my Dad and this guy. They would drink, I guess, and then we would go back to his place. My dad would pass out, that was his thing; he drank until he passed out. This guy would molest me as my dad slept. When my dad woke up, we would go home.

I told one of my sisters about my memories over the telephone. She and I were very close growing up, we are what they call Irish twins, our birthdays are a day apart and we are one year apart. I had never told her what had happened, which sat oddly with us both. She tried to help me piece things together, like maybe she had been away at gymnastics camp at the time or away at a friend's cabin. We spoke about all of the depressing poetry that I use to write and about the time I had attempted suicide in grade eight. I had collected pills that I found around the house over time. I had no idea what they were but I had this hard plastic container, filled. I remember the container was mauve and it had come in a package of tampons. I went into convulsions while I was sleeping and my sister woke my Dad and they took me to the hospital. I remember feeling that the nurses didn't like me. My Dad was very kind to me that night and my sister was by my side. I tried one more time, one night in the bath, but I'm not sure that I ever shared that with anyone. My mum gave me the silent treatment for weeks afterward. The entire event, my cry for help, was seen as a selfish act by her; so she punished me with her silence (My oldest sister had just survived a fight with stage four Hodgkin's so my mother thought I was trying suicide for unjustified attention).

On the phone, I asked my sister if she remembered the little pieces of cut paper, on which I wrote, I love you. How we would fold them up and hide them in Mum's shoes, and in her bags, we stuffed them into pockets of jackets hanging in the closet. We did it a few times. She remembered. Then, she asked me if I knew why. I did, It was my way of thanking my mother, for ending my outings with Dad and the guy.

Hastings Street, on the Lower Eastside of Vancouver, has a high concentration of chronically mentally ill people with debilitating addictions. For a few city blocks, the pavement is lined with hardship for the poor and homeless. During my commute to work, I drive along this road, and I have thought about where I might be had I not blocked and hidden away this trauma. I always give thanks for my life and those in it. I try to send out love as I pass, to all of the beautiful, but pain-soaked souls loitering there.

No one in my circle that I had shared this with ever brought it up again. I guess no one knew if it was an okay thing to do. Looking back, I wish that I had been asked more, I wish people had checked in to see how I was doing. I realize now, that no one could truly understand the enormity of how this trauma that had happened to me so long before, could enter every cell in my body and make me feel so toxic today, but it did. Even surrounded with profound love and receiving exceptional medical and professional care, the degree to which this experience damaged my person was enormous. I was fairly open to people, eventually, about being on antidepressants.

In my twenties, during a bout of depression, I went to a shrink for help, and that was not the best experience. The doctor gave me antidepressants and suggested that I try spirulina. One day while hustling to catch the bus, my entire body turned into a slow-motion robot. Everything in me slowed down, it felt like the world had sped up. During my next appointment, I told him about this and he said, 'Oh yeah, you shouldn't do any strenuous exercise". He asked me to bring photographs of all of my past boyfriends with me to my next session. I threw away the pills and never went back.

My family doctor referred me to an amazing psychiatrist, who helped me process everything. This became a safe place for me to leave soccer, playdates, birthdays, everything outside and only think about myself. Some sessions were more productive than others. I made good use of the kleenex box that was always sitting ready. I did most of the talking, I was never really told what to do. I was processing and she guided me through it, and once that was done, she listened to me figure out where I sit in this new place in my life and how to assimilate that with my old life. It is inevitable that once you go through a dramatic change of perspective, that other things around you will also feel the effect. Sometimes you represent something specific in a relationship, and once that thing changes, sometimes the relationship no longer has a purpose.

I needed to shed both people and behaviours. This decluttering of my life made room to allow for uninterrupted self-introspection. We lived in a small, sleepy little Coastal town, which helped me achieve this needed retreat. I started taking antidepressants. The pills were meant to improve my mood, allowing space for feelings of well being, and improve my energy level. It works by helping to restore the balance of certain natural substances in the brain. Serotonin and norepinephrine re-uptake inhibitors are used to treat depression, anxiety disorders, and long-term chronic pain.

On the medication, I could function again. I was able to go through the motions necessary to live my life. I had a few ugly experiences of being very ill due to the prescription, while out for a fancy lunch with a girl friend in New Delhi, India. On our crew bus, on the way to the airport in Sydney, Australia, I had to ask a colleague for a bag so I could be sick. It began happening to me all the time. The medication was difficult to take with my ever-changing schedule. Day becomes night and night becomes day in the life of a flight attendant. Eventually, after a long struggle to make my way through it all, I came to a place where I didn't feel the need for the pills anymore. They were starting to make my brain feel a little foggy and I would catch myself zoning out a lot. I had stopped seeing my psychiatrist regularly and needed another referral to see her again. Sadly my family Doctor suddenly passed away. I had been on the meds for a few years at this point and stopped them cold turkey when he died. This is not recommended, yet that is what I did.

Once I became aware of how my unacknowledged grief had affected my physical self, I began focusing much of my time alone on deep breathing and stretching. I didn't reach out for guidance or take a class as the journey felt too raw and personal for me to share openly. Instead, my bedroom walk-in closet became my refuge. There I could be alone with the door locked and it felt safe. My closet became the place was where some of the most transformative happenings of my journey occurred.

I spent much time deep breathing. I concentrated on filling air into the areas of my body that felt tense. I meditated and moved into poses that I didn't know as yoga poses, but that I felt the need to do intuitively. Once, while in a forward bend, I started convulsing. My entire self wretched, as if I was going to be sick. Instead, what eventually emerged, deep from my sacrum, was what felt like a large bubble. As it released itself from my mouth, mentally I had a flood of memories wash over me. Things that I had not thought about for years. Things, that I did not know I could even recall. The commonality in these thoughts was shame. Each memory that flashed through me held a feeling of shame for me. I regret not writing all of them down at the time, as they did not linger long. However, I do recall things, like a one-night stand that never should have happened, that sort of thing. I expelled something from deep within that had been causing me harm. I left my closet that day a little lighter.

By allowing myself the necessary steps to release these constrained feelings of shame and guilt, which had been thrust upon me as a child, and resonated unconsciously throughout later life, a space was created for my strength to grow.

My Dad and I live across the water from each other, three ferry rides apart, so it took me a long time before I was able to speak to him about all of this. I think a part of me was scared of what it might reveal. I wanted to do it face to face because I had to know definitively if he had any inkling what had been going on. I felt the need to see his eyes when I spoke. I was aware that my Dad had worked through his demons and had much regret about his alcoholism, and a part of me was hesitant to add to that regret. He came to visit, so I snuck the opportunity to whisk him off one morning alone. He protested at first, as I had sort of let on to his wife the night before that I had something to say. My dad isn't keen on getting into deep feelings often. With a story about needing toilet paper, I insisted that he jump in the car with me to go get some, and with him in his slippers, I drove us to the beach.

These things always feel so much larger than life before you face them, but there, in the car parked on the side of the road, it didn't seem like such a big deal. I told him what I had been going through. He hugged me. I cried.

He couldn't remember the guy's full name either but remembered the guy had a daughter.

Dad opened up to me about his relationship with his father. He told me stories about how much he missed him and how he wished he had his guidance throughout those years. My Dad told me that I would carry my trauma with me forever and for that he was sorry. He said that he too would carry it with him every day for the rest of his life, in a different way, but he too would carry this, with me, forever. That resonated and ended up being a big deal in my healing process.

Trusting my intuitive self gave me the courage to face the unknown. Even when I sprung leaks in my façade, I still had a choice. I chose to be honest with myself. Coping with the nuances of contradictory experiences of past and present is mentally stressful in itself. It requires energy and effort to sit with those seemingly opposite things that all seem true. I knew deep down I could not truly resolve this dissonance by letting the sleeping dogs lie.

By the time I had started to fall back into myself, the 'Me Too' movement was in full swing. Prominent people publicized allegations of sexual abuse and sexual harassment committed by powerful men. Sexual violence survivors all over the world joined hands and spoke about their experiences, many speaking for the first time.

Public perception shifted, this social movement made people more aware of sexual harassment and how casually it is often treated. By standing together as such a huge and diverse group, the tolerance of the abuse decreased and support for the victims appeared.

Every article that I read, every interview that I watched of a woman being brave and sharing her story, helped heal me a little more. Acknowledging and grieving for the pain internalized by that little pigtailed girl still in me was one thing, but recognizing that I had suffered, and that I wasn't alone, led to another level of acceptance. We are all worthy of love, including self-love. This affirmation released me from something that I didn't even know was holding me down. It re-innervated and brought back to life a strong conviction in me, understanding who I am, and how that knowledge has empowered every part of me. I no longer have a poor self-definition and I prioritize myself and practise self-care, which resonates with my children, my relationships, and beyond. I am a stronger role model and I am no longer easily bullied or manipulated.

Truth really did set me free. Free to love myself fully and completely.

Love gave me the tools I needed, to overcome the pain I held deep inside for all of those years. Allowing myself to listen to my authentic being, to be guided by my inner wisdom, I am able to look to the brightness ahead, rather than focus on the dark that no longer binds me.

I believe strongly that you too can choose success over adversity.

- ❖ Believe that you are capable of overcoming adversity, picture yourself doing just that.

- ❖ Give yourself permission to pause and bear witness to your life with complete honesty, over and over again.

- ❖ Trust your inner wisdom and allow it to act as your guide.

❖ Let go of what no longer serves you positively (whether it be an emotion, a behaviour or a person).

❖ Breathe Deeply and Release.

My healing process was like peeling an onion, with every layer I pulled back revealing another; each thin and translucent yet weight shedding as they fall away. PEELING Onions can make you cry, but THEY are essential parts of many dishes, and even good for you in surprising ways.

I was asked once if I was upset that it was me and not one of my sisters whom this had happened to. I thought it was an odd question. It is my story, it happened to me, I can't take that part of it away, so wishing it was different or projecting it on others does nothing positive.

My sisters and I use to joke about our family's ability to shroud issues, tuck them away under doilies, but I never thought about how that rubbed off on my life. I had love and many positive experiences in childhood as well, I learned to focus on that. Hiding this terrible experience wasn't the solution, as I eventually cracked and it all came oozing out anyway. I do feel that it kept the darkness deep inside, and allowed me to project light throughout my adolescence. If I had dwelled in the pain I experienced an earlier stage, I don't think I would have been brave enough to travel the world as I did. I believe that is the difference between me and the pain-soaked souls loitering on the lower East side, nothing more.

I am upset that I had to go through this dark period during precious mothering years, as it affected my ability to do everything that I had expected and wanted to do with my children. Yet at the same time, this experience made me into the person

I am today, and I love myself. I would hang out with me, and be my best friend. I don't know which part of me came out of that experience and all that unfolded afterward, and of course I wish it had never happened, but that girl and ALL that she has experienced, holding her, loving her unconditionally was what healed me and has made me who I am.

Writing this chapter was a challenge; I really had to push myself to do it. I backed out of an earlier attempt as it was just too much. For me writing this is also a part of my healing process, like a little finishing bow. If this writing can help anyone on their journey to overcome trauma, in any small way, as the words of many brave women gave me solace and strength, my heart will be full.

Life throws us many challenges, and sometimes when it's rough, I find myself making fists and curling up, sinking my chest in deep for protection. I am scarred, and aspects of my healing process will need to be revisited, and I will always have to be mindful to allow time for self care, but as far back as I can recall, every time I found myself making a wish, blowing out candles on a cake or tossing a penny into a wishing well, I always asked for contentment, and I can honestly say I have that now.

Today I am proud. Today I can say I truly experience living in the now, which has allowed me to feel more at peace with the past. I feel content.

About the Author
Carolina Parker

Carolina Parker knows that the journey to the destination is just as important to reaching its summit.

Born in Montreal to a large extended family who, in the late seventies, went their separate ways only to regroup in Vancouver, where she was raised.

As the youngest of three girls, she learned early to talk loud and fast to be heard. By the time she had finished Elementary school, she had moved houses eight times in three cities, giving her the perfect opportunity to hone her people skills.

After high school, she took a flight alone to Europe where she caught the travel bug, with very little money, a backpack and a huge smile she went on to the Middle East, where she visited a refugee camp in Gaza, Central America, where she taught English, worked in a Jazz Bar and showed real estate while learning Spanish, Africa where she participated in anti-apartheid rallies, and Asia, where she paid witness to Khmer Rouge victims. Carolina also learned Thai massage, to dive, skydive, and take the road less travelled ("Bad road good people, good road all people" became her explorational mantra.)

Carolina eventually settled in Vancouver where she fittingly became a flight attendant and mother to a ginger boy and girl. She and her husband continued to travel with their children until school and activities no longer allowed the time away.

Experiences while travelling the globe led her and her husband to start an eco-friendly company to help curb the number of single use plastics in our oceans and landfills. Together with their rescue cat and dog her family now live on the Sunshine Coast of British Columbia.

CHAPTER NINE

The Peace in the Puzzle

By Christina Kish Vince

"Ask, and you will see."

I'm sure that when I was a child, my mom used these words as a kind of 'dare' to keep us on our toes. Never, however, did I expect that I would learn to interpret and use these instructions to manifest amazing experiences in my life.

I've been a wife to my school crush for 20 years now, and a proud mama of two amazing, kind, and intelligent teenagers, who make my heart ooze. Well, except for when they are duking it out over electronics or giving me the gears about my neat and orderly ways.

As a regulated health care professional and a driven business owner for more than two decades, I absolutely love to mentor, learn, expand, and grow. I thrive when I can tap into my intuitive senses, and I never back down from a challenge. I suppose that is the 'Taurus' trait of stubbornness in me or simply my mother's DNA. At night, when my head hits the pillow, I know that tomorrow will be another triumphant day.

Why? Because... I can make a difference.

But, not so long ago, there was loneliness. Destiny and purpose were pushing me forward, yet my own resistance and hesitation were holding me back. This constant tug of war caused me to question my abilities and challenge my perceptions. It caused me self-doubt, self-criticism, and self-judgment, which triggered my indecisive decisions.

The Day Everything Changed

It was June of 2011, at the age of 37, when in one single sentence the world instantly swallowed me up. "Mom has stage four ovarian cancer", whispered my sister. Anger, disbelief, resentment, frustration, sadness, and fear ripped through my core. My heart sank and my thoughts scattered in endless directions in a matter of seconds.

I won't sugar coat it. I had several private meltdowns and temper tantrums that first month. I felt all the emotions from extreme bouts of rage to the complete numbness and disconnect of not giving a damn. Although I was furious on the outside and scared as hell on the inside, every morning I'd tighten my bootstraps, put on the fake brave face, and carry on. I, just like everyone else on the planet, had responsibilities to tend to. I had a never-ending list of duties, personally and professionally. I was now the exact portrayal of a working mom living in the "sandwich generation" caring for two young boys and two ageing parents at the same time. How could this possibly be the norm in my thirties?

In September, as I was sitting at London University Hospital in the Cancer Surgery Department with my stepfather, the surgeon emerged to confirm a large tumour had been successfully removed from my mother's abdomen. He continued, "But, unfortunately, significant cancer cells still remain that were too encompassing". Then, his following words would ring in my ears to this day, "We will see how many weeks or months your mom has".

In my mind, the countdown had officially started.

To make matters worse, eight months into my mom's illness, my stepfather's heath began to decline. His long-standing battle with diabetes, the added stress of my mother's disease, and her failing chemo trials had a rebound effect on his ability to cope emotionally and physiologically. As her struggle increased and her body's health deteriorated, so did his.

At the most extreme and consequential point, my father-in-law experienced his first stroke leaving him frail and weak. I had three parents, all terminally ill, in three different hospitals, in three different cities. My mother had stopped responding to all typical chemotherapy protocols. My stepfather was in kidney failure and having complications with dialysis. My father-in-law in critical condition.

My workday was constantly dysfunctional. I struggled to maintain a strong composure in front of my staff and clientele. I pushed myself to provide premium care in each interaction, all while my heart was breaking. I was distracted and overwhelmed. The ongoing health sagas consumed my very existence. I'd strategize health care and treatment options with my sister by phone, and then silently suppress my guilt for being unable to help out more. I would travel to attend medical appointments when I could, sometimes making the round-trip visit in a single day. Six hours of chemotherapy and six hours of driving on the most boring stretch of highway, away from my husband, my children, and my business.

One week before turning 40, while grieving my father in law's passing and the continuous, relentless decline of both my parents, I mistakenly believed things couldn't possibly get any worse. Then came the tragic call that my stepbrother had unexpectedly passed away from a seizure.

I was riding an emotional roller coaster and I desperately yearned for it to stop.

More Bad News

Two months later, in June 2014, my husband and I had just returned home from watching our boys play soccer when the phone rang. I could barely hear my mother's voice telling me that my stepfather was in the ER after having collapsed. His heart had stopped. After three separate codes involving resuscitation, the doctors mandated a DNR (do not resuscitate).

I frantically threw clothes in a bag, grabbed the car keys and was out the door in a flash for the single most stressful, lonely, and emotional drive I have ever experienced. I had absolutely no idea of the dreadful scenario I'd be walking into.

When I arrived, my stepfather was still alive. In fact, we would even celebrate one last father's day before his passing three weeks later. The next few months took a tremendous toll on my mother. Heartbroken, financially burdened, physically drained, and emotionally deflated, she lost her battle to cancer six months later.

By age 42, in less than thirteen months, I had buried four loved ones. I realized that I had gone through more stress, agony, pain, grief and sustained heartbreak than I could ever have imagined possible in such a short period of time.

My boys were now 8 and 10 and life was busy with sports, homework, meals, activities, and projects. I was working full-time hours, running my multi-disciplinary clinic, and managing a continuously growing staff. I was also a business partner to my husband's retail and online Amazon store, as he worked full-time as a truck driver by day, and entrepreneur at night.

It got to the point that every single time the phone rang, I'd hold my breath. My entire body would stiffen, and my heart would skip a beat. I was constantly on high alert. I realized that because of the upheaval I had experienced, my nervous system no longer knew how to normalize.

I was miserable. I felt abandoned and deserted by my pillars of support and the foundational roots of my identity. Feeling mentally exhausted, lethargic, emotionally drained, and physically tired, I began to shut down and check out. I couldn't even hold an engaging conversation with my husband. I felt shame and guilt for being a distracted mother and was losing my sense of patience and compassion in my business and with clients.

Silently, I was struggling to give a damn about life. It was time to take matters into my own hands by implementing stress management strategies and modalities that I now use with my clients.

Receiving the Divine Sign

Three months after my mom's passing, in a divinely timed ah-ha moment, I received the kick in the pants that I needed. A shiny, simple, divine sign appeared to remind me, that regardless of how bleak and overwhelming life can seem at times, there is a warrior strength within, waiting, and ready to triumph.

I woke up to the realization that my family deserved better from me, and that I owed it to myself to become stronger, more resilient and find my renewed sense of optimism. If I had any control over my future, it was now my time to take charge. In order to breathe, in order to thrive, I had to choose to lighten the load.

I made a clear decision to reduce my responsibilities, reclaim my personal power, take control of my schedule, and commit to seeking help to bolster my health and wellbeing. I also chose to embrace and be grateful for the amazing pleasures present in my life: my home, my husband, my children, the amazing opportunities that lay ahead and the wonderful memories kept safely behind.

It's terribly lonely not knowing your direction and having relationships end. I needed to embrace pieces of myself I didn't know were missing. It was time to stop reacting to my struggles and losses and recognize the potential I had within me. It was my time to shift perspectives to one of living and thriving. By practising the techniques that I facilitate with my clients today, I began to fall in love with the person that I used to be. In the midst of the grief and chaos, I had forgotten how to laugh, dream, and be spontaneous. It was now time to be present, joyful, and focus on creating new experiences and discover the gifts in each new day.

To transcend resentment, grief, and sorrow takes courage found from deep within. Our guards need to be let down, barriers lifted, and our wounds gently revealed. Healing is a process, and as such it requires an unwavering willingness, determination, and commitment. During it all, I gathered knowledge, insights, and tools that changed my life in many ways. My heart was opening. It was allowing me to discover the hidden treasures in my pain, and I was ready to release my regret for ignoring certain parts of my life.

The Nudge

After two and a half years, I was again immersed in daily routines, watching my boys flourish and develop, and having typical conversations at work. The moments of loneliness and sadness for my parents were reduced to holidays and birthdays and the deep heartache had softened significantly.

One particular morning I awoke with a startling voice in my head. It was crystal clear, unexpected, and even a little bizarre. I heard this voice say, "You need to know your dad". Now, this is not something that happens to me every day. In fact, it's never happened before. You see, I hadn't seen my biological father since I was 2 years old, when he and my mother had parted ways. My stepfather entered into the picture when I was four, so I don't recall missing my biological dad's presence as I was growing up. I had always known his name, and even had a couple of photographs stashed away, but never had I considered asking questions or reaching out. Graduations, major moves and relocations, my wedding day, and the birth of my children never triggered my willingness or desire to know more.

But on this particular day, the nudge was compelling... it was crucial to know my father.

Relentlessly, this 'thought' of needing to know my biological father continued to pressure me. After 42 years of separation from my father, I was actually curious about the other half of my genetic makeup. It persisted. It actually consumed my every thought as much as I was trying to bury it since I couldn't fathom experiencing grief anytime soon. The heart can only take so much.

But I couldn't turn it off!

I had no idea where to start my search for him, so I began with the obituaries. According to a search from 2015, my father was living in my hometown where he was listed as surviving his deceased sister. I was sitting alone in a parking lot when suddenly spontaneous courage came from within. I picked up my cell and began to 'cold call' every "Fiorino" in the 411 online search directory.

An elderly Italian woman answered my third call, and barely understood a word I said. As language was proving to be a barrier, in full panic, I blurted out "I think he is my biological father and I'm looking to connect". She didn't skip a beat and continued to misinterpret my every word. I hung up stunned and deflated, and unsure what my next steps should be. There were no other numbers to call, and if language continued to be a barrier, my quest might be a sinking ship.

Inspired once again, my next moves were divinely guided for the remainder of the night. Something deep inside of me knew that I had to succeed. Returning to the previous obituaries, I searched the next generation of listed family members and proceeded straight to Facebook. I sent out a dozen friend requests with a simple, direct, and to the point message. Unfortunately, several profiles hadn't been active in months or even years.

Shortly after I sent my final friend request, the anxiously awaited response came. I had named the responder's uncle. A flurry of messages with questions, details, and pictures passed back and forth. I was vibrating at a level I can't explain! Thankfully, the last message received was direct contact information. Propelled by a sense of urgency and a fearlessness that I had absolutely nothing to lose, I sent one last friend request and message before signing off for the night.

The Missing Puzzle 'Peace'

I awoke the next morning to a response that had my fingers trembling as I typed. I had connected with my formerly unknown, youngest sister. Her grace, patience, and immediate acceptance of me filled my heart and lifted a weight off my shoulders.

Nine days later as my father wrapped me in his arms, we held tightly to each other for what seemed like an eternity as tears filled my eyes. Years of silence and resentment vanished. In that instant, my soul ignited.

It turns out that my father had a huge Italian family and I have five more siblings! My first Fiorino Christmas with my new family was filled with laughter, storytelling and of course, his famous handmade lasagna. There was so much to process. I had progressed through life unaware of subtle wounds and false beliefs that challenged my existence, dampened my self-worth, and triggered my insecurities around trust and unconditional love. Now all of it was unravelling, comforting my heart and my soul. I felt immense gratitude that I wasn't too late in choosing this adventure. The missing puzzle piece needed to complete my family picture had been found.

Freedom is our choice

Two months later, my dad suffered a debilitating stroke. By this time, I had learned about the joy that he had experienced through travel, dance, fishing, cooking, and of course a little bit of gambling. In the short time I knew him, I could appreciate his humility and commitment to his family. I now also understood his decision to forego heroic efforts to add time to his life.

I shared a private moment with him in the hospital and with his hand tightly clasped in mine, I told him how especially grateful I was that he welcomed me into his life. I also expressed my regret about waiting over 40 years to locate him. And for the first time in my life, I whispered the words, 'I love you, dad'.

The day before his passing, we celebrated an early 70th birthday with a party at the hospital. We had a celebration of his life with family, drinks, food, cake, photos, and music. It no longer mattered what tomorrow would bring. It was about seizing this moment and honouring the choices we have the power to make regardless of our circumstances.

What I Learned

I understand and appreciate how this journey happened in a way that has led me to this point in my life. I also have the vulnerability to understand that every hurt and loss experienced along the way has coaxed me closer to greatness, passion and purpose.

I'm still a woman who occasionally stumbles, but who now has the tools, support, and the permission slip to move through adversities with more ease, grace, compassion, and unconditional love. I'm able to embrace the subtle gifts in expansion.

I learned to be F.R.E.E.

- ❖ Face it head-on (acknowledge the pain or adversity)
- ❖ Release what no longer serves me (limitations and old beliefs)
- ❖ Embrace what I desire and imagine (find my truths)
- ❖ Elevate to meet it (take action to achieve it with bold courage)

I appreciate where I'm at, personally and professionally. Through my work, I witness individuals craft their own realities and experiences. They repair fractured relationships, heal old wounds, and release limitations to manifesting dream jobs and healthy bodies. Doing and being whatever we desire is possible with courage, guidance, and a sense of purpose. Tragedies can define us, but the pain does not last forever. Freedom of choice is invaluable. I wish to inspire people to take charge because I understand that only choice elicits your new experiences.

Every day I'm reminded by the quote that hangs in my front foyer, "Life is about the journey, not the destination".

My daily journey continues with "Ask, and you will see".

About the Author
Christina Kish Vince

Born and raised in Woodstock Ontario, Christina Kish Vince is the founder and sole proprietor of Transform Uniquely and owns a holistic multidisciplinary practice in Leamington, Ontario. As a Wellness Engineer and Resilience Coach, she offers sessions and online group programs for those ready to take charge of healing their physical dis-ease and emotional pain. Christina's unique Bio-Integrative Mapping framework and collaborative efforts empower clients to navigate their journey to sustained health and wellbeing.

Christina, a Registered Massage Therapist since 1996, is known for her intuitive hands. She uses her extensive training and experience to assess and heal patterns of disturbance in the body. By facilitating the release of vibrational dysfunctions, due to traumas and imbalances that contribute to dis-ease, Christina guides her clients to experience the freedom to thrive.

As a lover of beach strolls, a packing wizard, a finder of dimes, and a forever student of "life", Christina understands that people experience struggles, challenges, and adversities in uniquely individual ways, which requires a transformative approach to healing. She systematically and holistically optimizes internal harmony of a person's body and mind, thereby activating healthy immune function and beneficial neurological responses to effectively combat stress and improve overall vitality.

With her unwavering optimism, combined with curiosity and compassion, Christina has been presented opportunities to assist the dying, work with newborn babies, and facilitate healing for a winning racehorse. Every 'body' is vibrationally unique, but the human archetypal design is undeniably universal.

Connect with Christina:

Book your free Intention Strategy Call or Vibrational Assessment by visiting www.transformuniquely.com or connect directly with Christina by emailing transformuniquely@wavedirect.net.

CHAPTER TEN

Trusting Your Body: Creating More Through the Subconscious Mind-Body Connection

By Amanda Piasta

Earlier today, I was driving home thinking to myself, "How lucky am I to have found this incredible human being that loves me for me, just the way I am? She is amazing in so many ways - the exact qualities physically, emotionally and spiritually that I have been seeking all this time. And she's been right under my nose." My heart felt like it was expanding in my chest and over-flowing with love and gratitude for the life I am living.

For how beautiful my current situation is.

For how incredible this love and support feels.

For how healthy my body feels.

122 | AMANDA PIASTA

For how clear and powerful my mind is.

I had a total 'tough butch' moment about an hour earlier when I had stood up from the rocky driveway after changing her car tires over to winter tires. Staring off into the orange, sun-kissed afternoon sky as the autumn wind blew the loose hairs of my ponytail across my face. Just by looking at me, you probably wouldn't think I'm the kind of chick who can jack up a car with a puny jack, kick loose the lug nuts with a cheap wrench, and swap out the tires, all on her own.

Not only have I manifested my dream partner into my life, but I also have unreal strength, health, and clarity. I like to practice eating wholefoods, cleansing, and longevity-style exercise to keep my body and mind sound. I even use Subconscious Imprinting Technique [S.I.T.] to break judgements, false beliefs, and other destructive behaviours, on a daily basis (more on this later). To top it off, I express my overflowing joy through song - I LOVE to sing and dance to express my happy feelings.

Just one year prior to writing this, I never thought that I'd be living in Kamloops, BC Canada of all places. Building a business that I'm completely passionate about, living with my 'forever love', my 'soulmate', the 'love of my life', if you will, and all the while, feeling like a superhuman!

But it wasn't always that way...

12 short months ago, I was living in North Vancouver with my now ex-wife. I was working a stable, corporate job as a Team Manager for Rogers Communications, one of the biggest telecommunications companies in Canada. I was really good at it, the pay was good, and my boss was cool.

My apartment was a big 2 bedroom with a 1.5 bath located in a desirable North Van neighbourhood. And since I'd lived there for nearly 8 years, it was still affordable (that's not a statement you'll hear many Vancouverites say).

My now ex-partner was beautiful with her golden Moroccan-kissed skin, bubble butt, and natural curls that fell perfectly on her shoulders. She's got a personality that people can't help but fall for.

I could afford to eat out at the local restaurants 3 or 4 times a week, or buy and eat organic at home if I chose....

but NONE of these things were feeding my soul. Quite the opposite, all of those things were sucking my soul dry.

I dreaded going to work, even though I made my own schedule. My feet, ankles, knees, back, and neck ached constantly... even when I would sit down all day (against company policy).

I'd wake up feeling that way, no matter how hard I tried to stay off my feet, lose weight, exercise, eat better, get massages, acupuncture, chiropractic work, and even sleep it off. None of those things worked, and to top it off, I would fight off a migraine almost every single day. I was pumping myself full of caffeine to keep going because my sleep was horrid and Advil because I was always in pain. I hated my body; I was overweight and could barely look at myself in the mirror without feeling disgusted.

When I would come home for the day, I'd have to clean up the messy house just to feel a sense of peace and order. Dirty dishes everywhere, clothes on the living room floor, kitchen table covered in literal garbage - I rarely had help doing this.

It was exhausting after a full day working and dealing with complaining employees, customers and the constant pain underneath it all.

When we were both home in the evenings (which was only a few times per week), my ex would take me out to dinner because I just couldn't muster the strength to remain standing to cook a good meal (something I used to enjoy doing). We'd only ever talk about work - we didn't have much else in common other than food. She'd foot the bill because that was her way of showing me she cared and because I was in debt up to my eyeballs despite making a decent salary.

We'd head home to our apartment only to crash in front of Netflix and then shortly after, into our own beds, in separate bedrooms. I couldn't even sleep next to her anymore due to being a terribly light sleeper and her wanting to fall asleep to a show playing on her laptop. This isn't a bash on her, it's simply my perspective of the daily reality I was living.

I'd listen to music, but with a blank stare on my face. I didn't sing. I didn't dance. I no longer meditated. I just couldn't, no matter what I did or tried. In fact, I barely left the house to do anything but work or get food.

I was completely unfulfilled. I craved a deeper connection in my relationship. I craved strength and ease in my body, to love it again. And I craved a heart-expanding career, something that would allow me to help people and impact the world at a deeper level.

I had thought that moving from sales representative to manager would solve my career issues. It didn't.

I thought marrying someone who was emotionally stable, financially stable, good looking, and that I considered my friend, would make me happy. It didn't.

I thought meditating, working out, eating whole foods, and dieting would make me feel well again, help me lose weight, and help me sleep better. It didn't.

I couldn't figure out why I couldn't make any of these work despite doing the "right" things, the "recommended" things, by all the doctors, experts and gurus.

I was SOOOO depressed. I wondered: "Is THIS what I have to look forward to for the next 60-something years of my life?" (I was 34 at the time) and "Will I even live that long at this rate?"

I thought about taking my life. Those thoughts scared the shit out of me.

It got to the point where I literally thought I was going to get cancer and die if I didn't change something. Something had to change. Anything.

You and Your Body Know Best

Finally, after consistently waking up in pain day after day, no matter what I tried...I broke. Emotionally, I broke down. My thoughts turned suicidal and I remember thinking things like "It would be easier to just die", "Is this all my life will be for the next 60 years? Even 20 years?", and "If I continue like this, I feel like I'm going to get cancer and die".

I was in such a deep depression and the only person I knew that I could confide in with these thoughts was my cousin, Vanessa. I reached out to her, even though we hadn't spoken much since I moved to Vancouver. We were super tight growing up and into our twenties. We'd tell each other EVERYTHING. No filters. So, I knew I could trust her with my secrets, dark thoughts, my depression, my pain, and my hole of nothingness without judgments.

Luckily for me, she responded immediately to my cry for help.

She's an Acupuncturist and a self-proclaimed "witch". She's always been my guiding light when it comes to holistic health and what she introduced me to, changed my life.

She quickly made time for me in her busy schedule and facilitated a S.I.T. (Subconscious Imprinting Technique) session on me over the phone. My body and mind released massive amounts of trauma, memories, and emotions that had been trapped inside for so long.

She used S.I.T. to pull out stuff that I was afraid to acknowledge out loud.

I am so grateful for that single session. From there, my mind began to rewire itself and I started to choose differently from ever before, rocking and shaking my life to its very core and everyone and everything around me (for the better).

The next 6 months of my life probably looked like a hurricane from an outside view. I gave 4 weeks' notice at my long-standing job (they'd want me to train someone to take over my position). I told my now ex-wife that I wanted a separation and that I was moving out of the city (we'd already been sleeping and living in separate rooms for over a year). I cried my sorrows in a heartfelt conversation with my parents, one like I'd never had with them before. They were fully supportive and offered me a space in their home (that's huge for a 35-year-old who's been out of the home for 16 years).

I was following MY truth. I was ignoring what everyone else thought I SHOULD do.

They thought I was crazy to leave a stable job with benefits.

They thought I was crazy to leave my marriage of 5 years because "it takes work to make it work" and "she's a catch."

They thought I was crazy to leave such an affordable apartment.

They thought I was crazy to live on the side of a mountain, in the middle of 'nowhere'.

I listened to my intuition, my gut feeling, and I made my dreams a reality.

I was a mountain woman. I was living in the beautiful wooded neighbourhood, Westshore Estates, on the side of a mountain hugging the Okanagan Lake.

I was reading, hiking, meditating, cooking, and eating whole foods every single day.

I saw the world in COLOR again.

I began to SING again!

Once I settled into this new life and my chronic pains began to subside, I had more time to pay attention to other parts of my life. My digital marketing (side business) was one of them. And although I was decent at it, I realized that I wasn't fulfilled with it and I wasn't prepared to go back to living a life of 'good enough' or mediocracy again.

The thought of continuing in digital marketing, web development, etc. made my body feel heavy. I'd always been a natural with tech so it seemed like the "logical" career path for me and what I had traditional, educational training in.

So I took a huge leap of faith, I maxed out my line of credit (I had no savings or income after leaving my wife, my job, and the city) and joined The Empowered Healers Academy (https://amandapiasta.com/sitinfo) to learn *Subconscious Imprinting Technique*. **The very healing modality that saved my life**.

It was completely illogical and seemed crazy because I'd have to drive 12 hours (each way), through the wintery, snowy, Canadian Rocky Mountains every week for the next 3 months to make this happen. Even the Academy asked me if I was truly committed because that's a dangerous drive to do so often in the winter and they were at capacity anyway. I knew I had to do it because every cell in my body **LIT UP** just thinking about it. They enrolled me. I went ALL-IN.

Over the next 3-4 months, I dedicated most of my time to learning and mastering the Subconscious Imprinting Technique.

I was the first in my class to start practicing on myself and others.

I excelled at it.

Realizing that my intuition was stronger and much more developed than myself or others had originally thought. I channelled healing energies and messages into my sessions with ease.

I now eat, breathe, sleep, and live S.I.T.

I haven't looked back since.

Creating New Patterns

Overcoming the pressures from family, friends, and society can be extremely difficult when those ideas, values and beliefs are ingrained into us at such a young age. It can cause the strongest willed person to make choices that do not align with their divine truth.

By receiving a Subconscious Imprinting Technique session and by implementing the suggested homework from my practitioner, I was able to overcome my chronic daily pains in my feet, ankles, knees and legs.

I was able to eliminate migraine headaches from my daily life.

I was able to fall in love with and honour my body again.

I was empowered to take a courageous leap into a brand-new career path.

I had the mental strength to manifest my dream partner.

I was now able to CHOOSE to be the best version of me, regardless of what others thought.

Healing the subconscious is deep stuff. Some things have been programmed and embedded so deeply, that it takes time and perseverance.

My healing process for this particular stage in life spanned approximately 6 months. Granted, it was over 6 years of accumulated and repressed emotions and trauma.

By the 3rd month, I had begun to make choices that would lead me to the healing environment that my body and mind so badly needed.

By the 6th month, my aches and pains had completely vanished.

I honestly believe that this type of healing is a life-long process. As human beings, we are constantly facing adversity and the more we follow our irrational awareness, the more magic we will create in our lives. This simple idea has been programmed out of all of us at a very early age and I am determined to help any willing human reinstate it within themselves.

What Does It Take to Heal the Subconscious?

I learned to talk to my body. I learned how to muscle test myself and how to strengthen my connection with my intuition. This is my secret weapon and one of the best resources I have to allow me to follow my 'gut feelings' or 'intuition' or 'awareness'.

It also took a lot of courage to make the choices that I knew were right for ME, but might affect someone else negatively. The fact of the matter is, I cannot control how someone else feels, reacts, or chooses. I can only control myself, MY choices, how I react, and how I feel. Courage is so important here because if, for example, someone feels sad because I did not show up to their birthday party (maybe intuitively I felt 'yucky' or 'heavy' about going), they are choosing to feel that way. But by being courageous with the choices I make; I can create more in my life. And so can you.

Being able to take a step back and self-reflect, without defensiveness or judgement, has been important in uncovering what else needs to be healed. "Triggers" are a great way to reveal these broken pieces. For example, if my partner tells me about one of her exes, and I feel triggered, I know there is a piece of me that needs to be healed. She hasn't done anything wrong, she's simply sharing a story of her past. For me to be triggered by that story shows that I have an inner wound that needs healing. Recognizing and acknowledging these triggers has been one of the easiest ways to overcome them.

Subconscious Imprinting Technique, also known as S.I.T. has been a pinnacle resource in overcoming any type of challenge in my life. Physically and emotionally. What it's allowed me to do is to rewire my subconscious to allow me to be open to more possibilities and more choice.

One of the most obvious resources in my world has been family. I know not everyone is close with their biological family and if healing the relationships with that family is not what will create more for you, remember that "family" is what you make it. It can be extended family members, neighbours, or friends. Although I had to swallow my pride and admit to my family that my marriage was failing and I needed to leave, without that brave step, I wouldn't have had their support and that would've made making the changes so much more difficult.

That brings me to the environment. Change of scenery, environment, or surroundings can have a huge effect on the physical and mental well-being of an individual. I can confirm this based on my healing experience. Taking myself out of the stressful, fast-paced city and plopping myself into the middle of nowhere, surrounded by nature and good-hearted people, allowed me to slow down and take the time I needed to heal the wounds I had endured.

Mind Your Business

By now I'm sure you've realized that I believe mindset is THE most important thing in overcoming adversity. However, this isn't all about "thinking positive" because when your mind is stuck in limiting or self-destructive patterns, it becomes difficult to be optimistic, or choose differently. There has to be a 'rewiring' or 'reprogramming' before you can truly move into the right mindset.

There's a lot of talk out there about "positive thinking", "manifesting" and the like that say *you attract what you put out*. And while I do believe that, a lot of us don't realize the subconscious thoughts we're putting out.

That's where S.I.T. comes in. I don't know about you, but constantly trying to "think positive" can be exhausting - why not just reprogram our subconscious mind-body so that it does it FOR us?

This is a huge factor in how I was able to overcome what I did and achieve what I have achieved.

5 Ways to Start Choosing Differently:

Choose a method to practice daily self-reflection --- There's no lack of variety in methods to achieve this; journaling, meditation, visualization, etc. My personal favourite is called the Brag Book. It works like this: right before bed (because your brain is going into Theta brain waves) write down the date and below it, as many things that you can think of that you are proud of doing that day.

Some examples:

"I ate a healthy breakfast today"

"I held the door for 3 people today"

"I supported my partner through a difficult phone call"

"I wrote a chapter of my book"

"I took a shower"

"I'm writing in my brag book"

Don't underestimate the size of the brag. Some days are difficult and simply bragging about getting out of bed can be a huge win for some people.

The more consistent you are with your brags (meaning, doing it every single day), the more you reinforce in your subconscious mind that those things are GOOD and that you want MORE of that. A simplified "sciencey" explanation of how it works is that we are giving mini dopamine hits to the brain when we do something good. That feels good to the brain. The brain will try to find ways (subconsciously) to do more of those 'good' things to get that dopamine hit again and again.

Lastly, beneath the brags, write down one intention for tomorrow. One thing that you want to do or achieve the next day. To take it one step further, you can optionally write HOW you plan to achieve that.

The idea behind setting an intention is that as you sleep, your subconscious will go to work trying to find ways or possibilities for you to achieve that.

Acknowledge your pitfalls --- This can be one of the most difficult things to do because no one wants to feel inferior, less than, or down on themselves. It's not about beating yourself up. Quite the opposite, it's simply about acknowledging the pieces that need healing. Writing this down, or saying it out loud can be very powerful for the healing process.

As I mentioned previously, self-reflection is an important resource in the healing process.

Pay attention to the things that "trigger" you.

What makes you feel emotionally ill?

What makes you feel physically ill?

What makes you fly off the hook?

Write them down, acknowledge them, and then move onto the next step to begin healing them.

Forgive yourself and others --- Forgiveness is a prickly topic for those who have endured great physical or emotional trauma. For example, if someone killed your child in a hit and run and was never persecuted for it, you may feel like you can NEVER forgive them. The truth is, forgiveness does NOT let someone else off the hook for the wrongs they've done but releases the negative feelings and emotions stored in YOUR mind-body that are connected to it. In turn, that takes back YOUR power, YOUR energy, YOUR light, and allows for healing. Forgiving yourself works similarly - you can't go back and change what is already done, so by forgiving yourself, you give yourself the freedom to choose differently going forward.

A few examples:

I forgive myself for believing _____

I forgive _____ for believing they had a right to _____

I ask _____ to forgive me for _____

I give _____ permission to forgive me for holding _____ against them

Remove and break down judgements --- When we have judgements about how something SHOULD be or how it SHOULD HAVE been done, we are cutting ourselves off from possibility. Projections, points of views, conclusions, expectations, and separations are also included in this section because they all cut us off from what else is possible.

Again, these things can be difficult to overcome on your own when they've been ingrained from an early age by parents, family, friends, and society and another reason to have help through a method such as S.I.T.

To break these down, or even just to realize that we have them, becomes important in the healing process and overcoming pain, trauma, memories, etc. because it opens up your world to other opportunities.

Again, there's always a choice.

When someone says "I HAVE to take my kid to soccer practice"

No, no you don't HAVE to.

"But I'll be a bad parent if I don't" is a judgement, a projection, a point of view.

If you were to have someone else take your kid to soccer practice one week so that you have YOU time, does that make you a bad parent? The answer is subjective based on your judgements, points of views and conclusions.

One person can answer "YES! You're not being the best parent because you're not 100% committed to supporting your kid!"

While another can answer "NO! You're allowing yourself the space to be the best YOU that you can be for your kid while still getting them to their soccer practice!"

What feels LIGHT to you? Follow that. You don't NEED to do anything in order to make someone else happy.

So, ask yourself, what else is possible that you haven't even thought of yet?

Give yourself permission to choose differently than you ever have before -- Again, easier said than done if you have destructive patterns and beliefs buried deep inside your subconscious. However, simply writing or saying aloud, "I choose to do _____, even though I'm afraid of who I will be when I do" is so powerful for the subconscious. When we begin to rewire the subconscious, our new choices become more 'automatic'. That is the goal of all of this repetitive work. Repetition becomes a habit, habits become a personality and personality becomes the subconscious, the subconscious IS our automatic systems.

Remove limitations, ask yourself: How much better can it get?

Living in Truth

What is "strength"? The ability to hold yourself together emotionally? The ability to lift 150 pounds?

I believe it is doing what is TRUE to the Self.

After going through these trials, and learning what I've learned, I know that I can trust my intuition and 'inner-knowing' more now than ever before. Following that 'awareness' is the light that leads me in the direction that creates more - always.

Why has following "TRUTH" been so important?

- ❖ It has allowed me to fall back in love with my body. Loving my body now means that I no longer cover-up pains with drugs, binge eating, binge-watching, sleeping, and other distractions. I literally talk to my body to find what is causing the dis-ease within so that it can be acknowledged, released, and healed.

- ❖ I've found my soulmate. A love so truly, madly, deeply that honestly has no words to fully describe it. It's a relationship that fills my heart, that lights up my body, that ignites my soul and I believe only transpired due to the self-healing I chose and continue to choose to do.

❖ Understanding and communicating my feelings have gone from bewilderment to completely natural. Even though there are still times where it's difficult to verbalize how I'm feeling, especially when I don't WANT to say what I'm feeling, I can recognize when it's difficult to verbalize and state that. Doing this helps in bringing it to the surface and has allowed me to create stronger connections with my partner, my family, and my clients.

❖ I am more open to receiving judgements and criticism from others. Receiving was a big struggle for me in so many ways and I see it in many of my clients too. We all want to receive more love, more connection, more money, more joy, more health...but we don't want to receive the other end of it, judgements, aloneness, debt, sadness, sickness. However, by allowing myself to receive aloneness, for example, I was able to focus on healing myself and becoming the best version of me to receive the love of my life.

❖ Regaining a sense of peace and happiness in my mind has been one of the most beneficial health factors in following my 'truth'. From severely depressed, with little to no energy to pull myself out of bed, to feeling excited to start the day, to being able to observe the vibrant colours of the trees, plants and flowers around me, to feeling so at ease and joyful, that all I want to do is sing and dance at any chance I get.

❖ Following my intuition or "truth" like a Boss has allowed me to create more in my life. An example is when I moved from the mountain to the city to be closer to my partner, B. I found an apartment that was perfect. It had everything I wanted, at a reasonable price AND it was furnished which was super rare for this city...but when I went to check out the space, it felt so heavy - like my body was going to explode...so I had to say no even though it was completely irrational and illogical. In turn, I ended up moving in with my partner (again, against all logic), and we were able to foster a much more beautiful relationship because of it. All because I followed my truth.

❖ I dropped my digital marketing and affiliate business that I had been building for 2 years to pursue my dream career in helping others heal their pain. It's allowed me to become a magnet for the things I desire, be a safe space for my clients to confide in and heal, and given me space to live a life with more time freedom.

The biggest lesson I've learned from living in my truth is that what other people think I SHOULD do is NOT always what will create more, even when it seems completely illogical or irrational to go against their ideas and suggestions.

What seems right, logical or rational is NOT always what will create MORE for YOU!

I've learned to trust the "heavy" vs "light", the "yuck" vs "ooooolala!", and the "something doesn't feel right" vs "I feel so fucking EXCITED!"

If you're facing a difficult or challenging time in your life, I recommend starting to use the "Brag Book" method I mentioned earlier in this chapter as well as my Subconscious Reprogramming template found at https://amandapiasta.com/resources to start moving towards what you truly desire in your life.

I know from experience (as you've read), that trying all the things on your own doesn't always work. So if you find yourself desperate to move past your pain in a holistic way, reach out to me for a consultation to see if you'd be a good fit to work with me at https://amandapiasta.com/schedule.

About the Author
Amanda Piasta

Amanda Piasta is a certified Subconscious Imprinting Technique (S.I.T.) prac-titioner and a holistic healing, self-proclaimed sorceress. She specializes in using S.I.T. to help high-vibe peeps naturally heal chronic physical pain. Amanda is passionate about holistic health and is always exploring new methods and techniques to help her clients and herself heal at a deeper level.

Pain Chasing, Acupressure, Energy Medicine, Reiki, Meditation, Chakra Balancing, Access Consciousness and Subconscious Imprinting Technique are just a few of the methods she implements into her healing practices.

Amanda is proud to be a part of, and support the LGBTQ+ community, as well as those from diverse backgrounds and upbringings.

Being tried through various adversities including, but not limited to, alcoholism, depression, chronic pain, persistent injuries, bankruptcy, poverty, and emotional abuse, Amanda can relate to clients on a deeper level. She offers support above and beyond what most practitioners can offer because of her experiences overcoming all kinds of traumas, memories, and events.

To work with Amanda, you can expect to be challenged physically and mentally in order to the get the extreme results that you desire.

Her methods are subtle and non-invasive and she brings non-judgmental care and love to each and every client despite their situation.

Connect with Amanda:

Schedule a consultation to discover the *root cause* of your pain at: https://apiasta.com/schedule.

CHAPTER ELEVEN

Reclaiming My Voice

By Wyetha Cox

Today I am a proud mother of two wonderful daughters and a great son who have grown up to be self-sufficient adults despite some of some of the negative environments that I grew up in. I have grown to be a strong, confident woman. Even though life has thrown me some curveballs, I managed to survive all of life's obstacles.

I can honestly tell you that it wasn't always that way because my early upbringing started with child molestation by a family acquaintance and that scarred my whole mindset as to if I would ever be worthy of being loved. My frame of mind was to take what was given to me even if it was degrading, humiliating, or verbally and physically abusive. My idea of what I wanted and what I deserved was so blurred that I could not see I was moving through life blindly searching for accreditation of who I was!

When I was first introduced to my abuser it was a really vulnerable time in my life and I needed someone in my life to take care of me since I literally felt like I was giving all of myself to my family's needs. The more I spoke with him, the more I felt like this might really turn into something permanent. I had gotten caught up emotionally in this false image of him that he had presented to me and I was so happy just have someone giving me attention that I missed all the warning flags that had started to appear. I couldn't see them because I was wearing my rose colored love glasses. It was so wonderful at first; we were spending time together and talking on the phone often but then the contact started to cool down without him saying anything to me about why, so I kept quiet to see if things would change. After several months, I finally built up enough nerve to speak to him about it and it was then that I realized that I had it all wrong, because in my mind since we had become intimate we were technically in a serious committed relationship, but that isn't how he viewed us. He felt like we were just "friends with benefits." That realization was devastating to me and I tried to let him know but I felt crushed. It was like another blow to my already fragile self-worth. It would turn out that we would only see each other on and off throughout the next couple of years.

Yes, later, I let my heart lead me back into a relationship with my abuser because I believed this was who I truly wanted to build a future with, and the heart desired him and the heart would regret it! My abuser once said to me, "How do you eat an elephant?" to which I replied, "You cannot", and he said, "Yes, you can, piece by piece."

In the beginning of the second try on love, it was great because I finally got what I wanted, how I wanted it. This is what I told myself until the tiny cracks started to form in our relationship. We would be spending time together watching television then

I might make a comment on a man I saw and he would say, "Oh that's right, every man you see you sleep with." The first time he said it I thought it was a sick joke, and I didn't respond but then the comments would keep coming out of his mouth, referring to me as a loose woman with no morals. After several months of the comments, I had had enough and when he said something again this time I turned to look him in the eye and said very sternly, "That is enough. Don't you try to tear me down anymore saying that stuff when you yourself aren't an angel because we both know you aren't a virgin!" Although that was the last time he uttered those exact words to me, after that he just chose another method to attack me.

The holidays had come and my Pastor and his wife invited me to a Christmas party at their home so I bought my abuser with me as my date. I noticed he didn't seem comfortable during the party but I had attributed it to the fact that he didn't know anybody there. The next day I called my Pastor to tell him how much I enjoyed the party and because we are good friends as well I wanted his opinion on his impression of my date. He said, "Well he seems like a nice person even though he is a drinker." He caught me off guard and I laughed I said that he wasn't. He said that there was no doubt in his mind that my date was a drinker. I told my Pastor that he used to drink but not anymore. He promised me that he had stopped drinking and I didn't notice anything different and then I thought about how he kept his distance at the party. My Pastor and his wife had been my friends for many years and they have never led me wrong, but my heart would not let me see another flag so I pushed it to the back of my mind. I never mentioned anything to him about it because I was not ready to admit that it could be a problem, and so talking about it would only make it real.

The next thing he started to use against me was arguing about little things that were always my fault. It got so bad at one point that whenever we had to go to the store, the whole time we were on the way there I was making a plan as to what I had to get and which aisle I had to go down just so he wouldn't argue with me that I took too long in the store. Sometimes, no matter what I did or how quick I was, he still would find a reason to yell and fuss at me. Then he would find ways to dangle his control over me since I didn't have my own car and I needed to depend on him to get places. I would call him in the morning to ask him to take me to the grocery store and he would agree and I would wait all day for him to come only for him to call me later to say he wasn't coming but maybe tomorrow. Also, he started wanting to know everybody I was talking to on the phone and questioning who I was spending time with... but still it wasn't enough for me to see the flags waving right in front of my face. I just kept taking whatever he dished out because in my mind we were meant to be together, so I was willing to put up with everything.

If I was truly being honest with myself, deep down I was unhappy, but I was not going to tell anyone, especially friends and family. Slowly things that were in the back of my mind would come to the forefront.

One evening, my son came to me and said that he needed to talk to me about something. He kept his head down while talking to me. My son began by saying, "Well, I talked to my teacher about how I would tell you this" and I felt bad that my son felt like he couldn't approach me about something. He then proceeded to tell me that the other night he was in the bathroom looking for something under the sink when, under a pile of folded towels, he found a liquor bottle that had been hidden. I was shocked but I immediately knew who would have done it. I quickly thanked my son for coming to me and telling me about what he found and then I told him to please do not hesitate to come to me about anything. I waited until my son left the room then I called my abuser into the room and when he stepped in, I closed the door and I warned him to not speak to my son after I spoke to him.

When I finished repeating what my son told me, he immediately went on the defense and he started to call for my son, acting like he was going to approach him, and I had to make a stand to him that he better not say anything to my son. I also told him if he wanted to continue to come over to my house, he better not bring any more alcohol into my house. Now I was being forced to think back about what my Pastor had told me about him, and so it was sinking in that he did still have a drinking problem.

While I was still trying to figure out how I let myself get caught up in this mess, I discovered that I was pregnant. The ironic thing about this messy situation is that it was the first time that I was pregnant and the father would hang around to be in the picture. This was his first child so he was excited, but I was nervous because I was not sure if I could depend on him to be there during this complicated pregnancy. I thought that things would ease up between us since I was carrying his child, but things went to a whole other level. He decided to tighten the noose around me by becoming more controlling by trying to tell me how what I needed to do after our baby was born. He was stressing me out so much that it caused my blood sugar levels to rise and the doctors were so concerned that they decided to hospitalize me so that they could get my levels back in control. After returning home from the hospital everything seemed like it was going well until my abuser called me the day after Christmas to tell me his mother was sick and to ask me if I would come over to help her. I agreed and I told him to call me when he was outside. When I hung up the phone I proceeded to get the children dressed and we waited on my abuser to pick us up. He called to say he was outside, so we walked out to his car and I was so busy getting the children loaded into the car that I did not pay attention to his behaviour. We were on our way to his mother's house and all of a sudden he started saying how "I was nothing but a no good woman" and so, I turned to him to tell him not to speak to me that way, especial-ly in front of my kids. He kept talking about me like I was noth-ing then he called me a b**** after which I informed him that I had changed my mind and to take me back home. He said, "No I'm not taking you back because you told my mother you were coming over to help her, so I'm taking you to her house." I turned to look at my children and I saw the look of fear on their faces. My son moved his feet which caused a noise and I looked down to see beer cans. With my heart racing, I was de-vising a plan of what I was going to do as soon as my abuser pulled up to his mother's house. We pulled up to the house and as soon as the kids and I stepped out of the car, I told my son to take his sisters up to the convenience store and that I'd meet them there so we can catch a cab back home. I was in the middle of handing my son his baby sister when my abuser grabbed me by the neck and started to choke me right in front of my children. I was trying to fight him off of me, which loos-ened his grip on my neck. I told my son to go do what I told him to do but before he could leave, my abuser grabbed the baby out his arms and headed for the house, so I told my son to go on as I headed into the house after my baby. When I got inside the house, I told my abuser that I would go upstairs and apologize to his mother and tell her that I couldn't stay. While I was up there I called a cab, then came downstairs to get the baby. He refused to let me have her so we ended up tussling back and forth until he loosened his grip. I pulled her with all my strength out of his arms and then ran to the cab where my children were waiting for me.

After this horrific incident, I sought advice from my Pastor on what to do. When I prayed what my Pastor suggested, I began to see some ugly truths about him that I was blind to before.

After that day, I was on my own. The only time I would allow him to come over is when he would say he wanted to spend time with his daughter. One morning when he was at my house, my phone rang and he answered it. It was a man calling for me and he got angry. I told him it was just a friend. I told him not to pick up our daughter from daycare today because I plan to pick her up after work. He agreed and then left while I finished getting ready for work. After work, I went to pick up my daughter from daycare but was informed that she had already been picked up by her father. I was livid! The drive to my house was not a pleasant one at all because all could think about was what I was going to say to him for totally disregarding my request. When I pulled up to my house, he comes answering my door like he lives there (another thing that I told him to stop doing and despite what I insisted on he still kept doing it.) My abuser then tells me that he's cooking dinner and that he will bring a plate when it's done. All I wanted to do was scream at the top of my lungs but I didn't want to cause a scene in front of my children. So I waited but I was worried because he was acting really strange.

I went to my room to change out of my work clothes and to wind down before eating dinner. I was also I was trying to calm myself down and prepare myself for a discussion with him about totally dismissing things that have asked him not to do. Finally, he brought my plate of food into the room and served it to me. I interrupted his meaningless chatter to ask him why he picked up our daughter today after I asked him not to? He responded by saying that he wanted to help me out. I reminded him I had plans but he just did what he wanted regardless of what I asked and he just stood there looking at me. His conversation and his mood seemed to get dark as he brought up the guy who called me on my cell phone and then he made a slight threat toward me. This wasn't the first time but I was scared. I continued to eat my dinner, while formulating a plan should he act upon his threat of physically hurting me. My abuser began to pace back in forth as if to build up the nerve to really harm me. It was only my baby girl, myself, and him in the room so I told myself the only protection I had to defend myself and my baby was the china plate I was eating off. My plan was to swing the plate at him to defend myself if he came towards me The next thing I knew, he lunges toward me and puts his hands around my neck just like before! This time, I instinctively swung the china plate toward his face and it cut him across his forehead which caused him to release his grip on my neck.

He grabbed our daughter close to him and told her "Look at what your mother did to me" as he let the blood from his forehead drip on her. Before taking a second to think, he lunged forward towards me again and I told him that I was going to call the police if he put his hands on me again. As he was trying to put his hands around my neck I was already reaching for the phone to call the police. As I was waiting for the police to arrive, my abuser told me that I'll be going to jail because I cut him. I realized he was right so I made a call to my godmother to be prepared to come to get my children should he press charges for his injury. When the police arrived, they asked if he wanted to press charges against me, and he said yes. It didn't matter that he tried to strangle me once again; all that mattered was that he was bleeding and he made it sound like I was his abuser. Luckily, he changed his mind about pressing charges, and he went to the hospital to get stitches. My children had been in their room with the door closed while the police were there and I went to them to reassure them that they would not have to worry about him coming around anymore.

When I finally got out of that mess, I had to educate myself on my rights through a very antiquated legal system that was set up through a male-dominated court system that had the right to deny you protection unless actual violence had taken place and even a piece of paper couldn't necessarily protect you from your abuser. I would take many trips to the courts due to my case being continued. The best part of the process was I learned about an organization that offered counselling services and emergency cell phone services while my abuser was stalking me. They also had a facility that was used for court-appointed supervised visitation. Through the counselling, I was able to understand the cycle of abuse, the warning signs, and how to prepare an emergency plan to flee.

It would take years to fully feel like I was free of the mental and physical scars of the abuse and the residue it left behind.

I had to completely change my way of thinking about myself so that I finally realized I am a complete woman even if I do not have a man in my life. My life was worth more than allowing a man to tear me down verbally and physically hurt me.

I put everything into working hard at my job so that I could make ends meet. My abuser stopped working and didn't pay any child support. I made up my mind: I wasn't going to let my children down ever again.

I feel like my mental wiring was screwed up from my early childhood which caused my self-esteem to be very low. It was only with much prayer that I was able to get a stronger mind-set to finally overcome some major adversity that happened in my life.

Whenever you are in the middle of a crisis, seek help from your higher power for the strength to get through it. You must look at the adversity as a temporary setback that you will over-come. Always remind yourself of all the positive times that you have had in your life. Your overcoming the adversity could help someone else who may be going through the same thing because many times when a person is in the middle of a situa-tion they feel alone and that they are the only ones dealing with that situation.

I found out through this that I was quite capable of doing things on my own with the support of true friends and family. The more I was able to accomplish, the more my confidence was starting to build up, then I started to appreciate who I was without being desperate for a man to complete me.

I learned that there is a difference between being lonely and being alone. If you are with someone who doesn't make you feel better about yourself, then walk or run away from that person quickly and please don't think that things will get better if you wait.

My advice to someone in the middle of an abusive relationship is to look within yourself and find that center when you felt sheer joy and happiness then try to remember what gave you that sense of excitement. Now let go of any weight that is hindering you from feeling that special way in the present moment.

I am now walking in my victorious life happily now after all the pitfalls of life - and so can you!

About the Author
Wyetha Cox

Wyetha Cox is the daughter of the late Blanche E. DaCosta and Wilbert Cox and grew up in Washington, DC as the eldest of two children.

Wyetha has worked in the customer service, banking, and governmental contracting industries. She is a change agent that worked with a grass root advocacy organization that fought for fair housing practices, helped with lead testing in low-income areas, worked on raising the minimum wage, voting rights, and against predatory lenders, etc. While apart of the organization Wyetha was selected to be a community leader which sparked a spirit of activism within her.

Wyetha's mission is to give back to the community by enriching other women by sharing resources and experiences that can empower them to live a victorious life! She wants to show them that they can be successful in their personal and professional endeavors by overcoming any past obstacle.

Wyetha is the proud mother of a son and two daughters and resides in Odenton, Maryland.

Wyetha is the author of a memoir as well, entitled "Please Abuse Me...Said No One" to be released in 2021.

Connect with Wyetha:

www.wyethaecox.com

CHAPTER TWELVE

Living and Loving Heartfully

By Pia Antico

I have been saying 'YES' to a lot of things lately, co-authoring this book being one of them. Not so long ago I was not as quick with the fearless 'yes giving'; for a great deal of my adult life, I struggled under the weight of my survivor badge of honour. A badge that kept me trapped in the remnants of events long passed.

I can hear you ask, "surely seeing yourself as a survivor is better than seeing yourself as a victim of the trials and tests you've been through?" Well, by the end of this chapter I hope to show you that it's not so much about what stories you tell yourself that's at issue, but rather the problem lies in believing you are the stories you tell yourself at all; regardless of whether you paint yourself as a hero, villain, or victim.

My name is Pia Antico, formerly identified as a "three near deaths before 30, two abusive marriages, and a major head injury life rebuilder." I inspire and support women who want to access their innate Spirit-led wisdom so that they can live and love heartfully in the present moment.

The moment I decided I no longer wanted to identify as a 'survivor' was at my older brother's 50th birthday celebration. When the birthday boy delivered his witty and poignant birthday speech, thanking and acknowledging the important people in his life, when he got to me he commended my strength and resilience having survived the kinds of trials that many would have buckled under.

Now, I know he said this with immense love, pride and awe of me, but at that moment I realized that when people think of me I don't want it to be by the numerous devastations and life-threatening events that happened to me in the first half of my adult life. Surely there was more to my existence than a list of negative events? This reflection started me on the journey to seeking out what made me and others experience our lives as we do, what makes us struggle with letting go of past traumas and have us worrying about our unknown futures? Is there more to us than a collection of thoughts, emotions, and actions? I certainly hoped that I was more than the sum of my thoughts.

Where did my seemingly unwavering resilience come from in the face of abuse, chronic illness, major brain injury, miscarriages, moving continents, and returning to Australia penniless, homeless, unemployed, sick, and traumatized? Believe me, there were many points through these events where I almost lost all hope and found myself balled up weeping and screaming into an abyss begging for an end to it by any means necessary; to the point of considering ingesting the bottle of opiate painkillers freely gotten over the counter in a Pakistani pharmacy. It was certainly a plausible way of exiting the abusive marriage and would relieve me of my weakened physical condition that had developed due to the food, water, sanitation, and anxiety of the marriage.

Where did I draw the strength to keep moving beyond the fear, hurt, anger, resentment, and confusion? I wasn't able to 'logic' my way through this roller coaster of a life.

Every so often, out of nowhere, I would realize an urge within me to keep going, a flicker of hope that propelled me forward into the unknown. For an exceptionally long time I did not know what this urging was and more often than not I would rationalize it away at my own expense. My three degrees in Psychology with a focus on empirical methods and theories gave no credence to a level of awareness separate to our brain biochemistry and cognitive functions, so I started to look for the roots of this inner awareness on a Spiritual path through Buddhism, Sufism, and New Age Sacred Feminine practices; anything to try and plug myself into the Universal energetic matrix that enveloped me and proved that I was far more than my personal thoughts.

However, I came to see that intellectually understanding that I was more than the sum of my thinking, was not the missing piece I needed to enable me to fully release the past stories of pain from burdening me in the present moment.

Even though I knew in theory that I was a Spirit being made of the same radiant, vibrant & expansive energy of the Universe with access to infinite possibilities & abundance, I found myself stuck on my lounge mentally summoning my then-husband on the other end of the couch as I replayed the arguments trying to understand what actually happened and why.

"Today, I let go of the ashes, let go of the disappointment, let go of the blame. Take those ashes, your broken dreams, your hurts, your failures, even your questions; put them in God's hands and say 'God it was not fair, they hurt me, my dream did not work out but I refuse to live life looking in the rearview mirror. You promised me beauty for ashes, so right now I am releasing the bitterness, I am forgiving the people that hurt me and I am letting go of the disappointments.

Letting old doors close so I can walk through the new doors you have ready to open for me. Alhamdulillah! Ameen."

-Diary entry from March 30, 2017, four months after returning back to Australia from Pakistan with nothing but a suitcase.

As it turned out, the realization and lived experience of this prayer did not come to bloom until October 23, 2020 [as I am writing this story]. What stands out in this prayer, the root obstruction to the experiential shift of wholehearted release, is that I was still stuck in believing that the other people were the cause of my pain and suffering and thus setting me up for three more years before I truly can say that with love, compassion, goodwill borne of humility and forgiveness that I am able to release the stories of suffering and survival. The truth is, in every situation each of us was hurting ourselves by getting caught in our ego conditional love and denying ourselves the ability to connect Spirit to Spirit (our true selves). I can't help but look back with compassion, humility, forgiveness, and a tinge of sadness for what we all lost by not being present to our vibrant infinitely loveable selves.

The Path to a Paradigm Shift

I found myself trying to disrupt the mental chatter with meditation and prayer, but it seemed that the more I tried to push away distressing thoughts and feelings of anxiety, they just came back as strong as before. Distraction, analysis, and trying to control my thinking and feelings did not help me to move beyond my survivor identity. I intellectually knew there was more to the Universe, and that technically it was meant to be available to me, but really feeling this in the core of my being eluded me.

That was until I was given the greatest blessing in my life, the opportunity to learn about and certify in the Inside-Out Paradigm.

The Inside-Out Paradigm (Sydney Banks, 1970) is the missing piece that enabled me to shift from intellectually understanding the source of my resilience to internalizing this TRUTH experientially. A shift that has underscored my ability to face the ongoing tests and trials of life with hope, compassion, patience, and curiosity.

Since my return from Pakistan on December 1, 2016, after leaving my abusive marriage with just a suitcase of Desi clothes, I came back to Australia with no money, no job, no home, poor health, grief, shame, regret, and strained relationships with some family members.

Since December 2016, I took a leap of faith and became a Relationships Reset Mentor. Starting my business Essential Awakening Mentoring provided me with another platform for the realization and releasing of old stories of worth like, "if I invite them they won't come" that got in the road of me daring to put a price (value) on my services. When you love yourself fearlessly, you can put yourself in comfort-stretching growth opportunities like getting on camera and writing this book, laying my life out without being concerned with being understood or meeting other people's approval.

I have stared down the very real possibility of being homeless after having rebuilt my life and securing an apartment that I newly furnished.

So yes, the roller coaster has been wild and though the outer circumstances may look a bit similar today being technically in an insecure financial state, but *my experience of it is totally different!*

Do I still have moments of fearful ego thinking? YES

Do I sometimes not experience the protection of God? YES!

But those moments pass because I do not let my ego thinking run with it.

Because I can see clearly that it is not my efforts that secure the outcome, it is God's mercy, and His mercy comes in forms beyond my limited understanding. When I used to think that there was only one logical way for a situation to be solved, and when I kept being thwarted in solving my problem, I would get sick with worry, self-doubt and anger. When I saw that I needed something (e.g. to not become homeless due to the lack of income and drained savings) I continued looking for a job, *but,* I opened myself to other solutions, I kept seeking from God to show me the way and I kept taking a deep breath when the fear rose and I started to get into my thinking.

As it turned out, a solution was found. I am still in my apartment with the help of my family. After all, accepting help is at

SHINE | 163

the core of self-love. The solution yet is not from my own hand through a full-time salaried job or an 8-figure Mentoring Business. But that is OK, God has me where I am meant to be and doing what I am meant to be doing. When I focus RIGHT NOW! This second, I have a home, I have food, I have clothes, I have health enough to be able to get healthier. Right now, I have what I need Alhamdulillah! I know that in the next second God will give me what I need in that second. So, I do not have to spend this second worrying about the next. Life has become hopeful, curious, a bit absurd, and rather amusing, it turns out my Universal alignment is guiding other women to live and love fearlessly. Even after two abusive marriages, I am not as cynical about men and relationships as I used to be. This is because I know where my emotions come from and I know that my Spirit Self is love. I don't need to look elsewhere to find love or force someone to try and fill me up with love. Now, that is liberation! The other people can jump up and down making a disturbance but I don't need to let it affect me. If another man were to try and treat me in a way that is counter to Universal harmony, then I know that my Spirit wisdom at that moment will guide me to the most appropriate response. I will be able to do that because I won't get caught up in egocentric thinking where I am concluding my worth based on their behaviour.

I am basically content and chill for the first time in my life and that's without having to have my external circumstances change in some idealized way. The unknown is still unknown, but I am okay with paddling in the spaces between.

The 5 key guidelines for living & loving heartfully

1. We are living in the feelings of our thinking 100% of the time

Have you ever felt, said, or thought:

- ❖ He/She made me so angry.
- ❖ My job is pissing me off.
- ❖ I am going to go crazy if the kids don't stop making so much noise.
- ❖ I'll be so relaxed when I finally go on vacation.

Do any of these statements sound familiar to you?

Can you see that all these questions & statements have one thing in common?

At the core, they assume their experience is caused by the situation or other person. That something needed changing outside of themselves before they could be okay. But I have found that isn't the case... we are living in the feelings of our thinking 100% of the time. Of course, events happen and people do stuff; but it is not to us. It's our ego fear-based thinking that makes us personalize the actions of others of the situations that happen, and thereby add an unnecessary layer of thought-created suffering that closes us off from our present centred heartful wisdom response. If you find yourself stuck in your thinking about a person or situation, take a step back, a deep breath, and release the thinking with forgiveness and compassion for all involved. Know that if you do need to take action that the solution will arise from your innate Spirit-led wisdom; not from any amount of ego-based thinking.

2. Everyone has their own reality, no need for defensiveness or judgement

At the core of so many arguments and misunderstandings is the false assumption that others should see the world as we see it, "If they loved us they would know what I want"; how many times have we all thought this at one time or another?

But here's the thing, we all have our own unique thought created reality, none of us will ever experience the same event in exactly the same way. Think of going to the movies in a group, you are all watching the same movie at the same time, subject to the same environmental conditions; each person will walk away with a different experience. One may have focused on how cold they were in the cinema, another may have been preoccupied with other worries to have paid attention to the film, all while you totally loved the film, fully engrossed and gorging on buttery popcorn. Everyone is responding to their thinking at that moment, so if someone says or does something you didn't expect or disagree with, that's okay. You don't have to agree or even understand another person in order to maintain a whole-hearted Spirit-led connection.

3. We are Spirit beings having a human experience

At first, I thought mentioning this fact was too obvious. Doesn't everyone realize this truth, just as I do? But then I remembered 'separate realities' and that there are many people in this world who are convinced by the arguments of a purely material existence. The only reality being one that is measurable. For such people, there is only this physical world and they are merely the sum of their thoughts, feelings and actions. And as such, when things go wrong, they can struggle to make sense of the trial, let alone find hope within the struggle. I know that when I was stuck in trying to think of a solution to my financial struggles and kept facing job rejections, the hopelessness and worry set in quickly. But, with an insight into an existence greater than myself and the physical world, knowing that I am more than the sum of my thoughts gave me the resilience, hope, and gratitude needed to navigate my struggles.

The difference as I see it is one person being grateful that they had a glass of water to quench their thirst, while I am grateful to God/the Divine/Universe for providing me with the glass of water.

4. **The past is dead & the future is unknown, so remain in the present**

The only reality is the present moment, the past is dead, and we only bring it to life in our thinking in the present moment. Using thinking that is inaccurate and incomplete at best, there is absolutely no point in ruminating about the past and rehashing stories in your head. The past can't be changed, all you can do in the present moment is release the past with forgiveness and compassion for all involved knowing that everyone was doing the best they could with what they knew. As for worrying about the unknown future, maybe ask yourself why are you assuming catastrophe rather than triumph? God, the Universe, and your Spirit are all made of limitless abundance, radiance and love; everything that happens in life is for our ultimate benefit, even those times of loss and sadness. Everything that is meant for us will come to us and all that is not meant for us will miss us. Our job is to show up in the present moment willing to listen to our Spirit-guided wisdom and respond with an open heart.

5. **Our factory default setting is Love, so be the love that you are**.

*"Those that go searching for love only make
manifest their own lovelessness, and the loveless never
find love, only the loving find love, and they never have
to seek for it"*
-D. H. Lawrence

Our books, music, and movies constantly tell us a story of seeking love outside of ourselves and finding that one person to fill the perceived emptiness inside ourselves. And from this misunderstanding, we put pressure on others in our lives to fill us up and complete our lives. But this is wrong, we are not empty, and we don't need anyone to fill us up (not that they can anyway). When we realize that we are Spirit beings, and our nature is unconditional, radiant, and ever-expanding love then we don't go in search of what we already have in abundance. We are free to be the love we are in every present moment to all those who come onto our path, starting with ourselves.

Today, my purpose and passion as a Relationships Reset Mentor is to guide women back to their innate heartful wisdom whenever they get stuck in their ego thinking and lose sight of the infinite possibilities available to them in the spaces between thoughts. I help women to find ease in uncertainty and to open their hearts to the limitless abundance of the Universe by releasing the stories they are telling themselves with humility, forgiveness, and compassion; so that they can experience their lives with calm, clarity, contentment no matter the situation.

As for that Survivor Badge of Honour weighing me down, I unpinned it and lovingly wrapped it among my box of mementos of times long passed. I dance in the liminal spaces between being and becoming these days, free from the yoke of personally identifying with the events in my life.

Are you ready to live & love fearlessly at this moment?

About the Author
Pia Antico

"In the middle of a storm, it is possible to find peace & strength when we tap into our innate Spirit-led wisdom and step heartfully into the present moment."
- Pia Antico

Pia Antico is the Founder of Essential Awakening Mentoring, a Relationships Reset Mentor & Author. She supports soulful women in shifting their experiences of their relationships with self & others, using her signature AWAKEN the joy within© model so that they can live & love heartfully from their innate wisdom in their present moment. This allows her clients to respond to any situation with calm, clarity & confidence; enabling them to live life joyfully & experience greater closeness in all their relationships.

Pia holds three degrees in Psychology, Counseling Training, and Back to the Fitrah Certification in the Inside-Out Paradigm. Additionally, she learned how to thrive after two toxic marriages and following an accident that left her with a life-altering brain injury; all while she raised a resilient, courageous, & creative daughter who has now stepped into her own light & soulful marriage.

Connect with Pia:

https://www.linktr.ee/RelationshipsReset